Walking In Teesdale

By

Keven Shevels

TRAIL GUIDES
publications

First published in Great Britain in 2014 by Trailguides Limited.
www.trailguides.co.uk

ISBN 978-1-905444-57-1

The route diagrams in this book are based upon 1925-1940 Ordnance Survey One-Inch maps updated by field trips and site visits.

Trailguides Limited
35 Carmel Road South
Darlington
Co Durham DL3 8DQ

Cover design by Steve Gustard
Artwork by Trailguides Limited

CONTENTS

Cover photos.
Front cover. Following the path above The Trough. Walk 6. Citron Seat and Seven Hills.
Back cover. Crossing the Gill Beck. Walk 9. Banks of the Greta and Grey Stones.

INTRODUCTION

1. Introduction

The River Tees is one of the major rivers of the north and in it's upper reaches is a heaven for walkers. Here the river descends from the high Pennines, flowing between high moorland peaks as it makes it's way down the valley. Then as the hills gradually lose their height and become less stern, the wildness that characterises the upper dales gives way to pastureland, woodland and pleasing riverbank walks.

However, don't just think of Teesdale as the main river valley. The major tributaries of the Tees all flow in from the west, these being the rivers Balder, Lune and Greta, while on the eastern side an ample number of smaller becks and streams flow in giving a number of hidden side-valleys that can be a joy to explore. Together with the main river valley, this presents a vast area to walk in for those willing to step away from the popular Pennine and Teesdale Ways.

While there are elements of both these national trails included in the routes of a couple of these walks, in the main this guide book takes you away from the more frequented areas and presents a mixture of countryside. Here you can venture onto the wild open moors, explore wooded side-valleys and stroll along the riverbanks of the rugged but beautiful River Tees itself.

But the countryside of Teesdale is not just about the scenerary, splendid though that is. Like many upland areas of the north, lack of cultivation and ploughing has meant that the hills have retained much of the history that has been lost on lower-lying ground. If you know where to look, then a walk through Teesdale can be a fascinating education. In many ways Teesdale is one of the original 'open-air museums'.

2. Access & the Right to Roam

Teesdale and it's tributary valleys presents a large area and a mixture of landscapes for the walker to explore. This, in turn, also gives a corresponding mix of access rights to use. In the lower, cultivated levels around the sides of the valley and the valley floor itself, access is legally restricted to public rights of way such as footpaths and bridleways and this is reflected in those routes contained within this book that cross this cultivated farmland. The open moorland on the fringes of the dale plus the high hills that straddle both sides of the upper dale have, in the past, had the same restrictions placed on them. However with the implementation of the Countryside Right of Way Act 2000 in 2005 and the "Right to Roam" this has now all changed and certain upland areas of this part of Teesdale that were once closed have now become legally accessible to the walker. This legislation allows walkers the right to roam at will over "designated access land" without the need to be restricted to official footpaths and bridleways.

The details that accompany each of the walk descriptions will provide information as to whether the route uses rights of way or crosses open access land.

On the new editions of the Ordnance Survey Explorer maps, this new access land is marked with a light yellow coloured background and at the entry points to this land, the stiles and gates carry the new "access land" waymarking symbol of a brown stick man in a brown circle.

With the right to access has also come responsibility and the walker is expected to observe various limits and restrictions that are placed on their activities at certain times of the year. The landowner and/or farmer has the right to exclude access for up to twenty eight days per year and this is normally applied between May and early July to coincide with the breeding season of the ground-nesting birds on the moors. Where they are known, restrictions that may impinge on any given walk are shown in the details for that walk. However, don't take it for granted that these are going to be accurate, as each year these restrictions may change. Always check any notices that are placed at the access points for any restrictions. To find out more on the `right to roam` and whether any general or specific restrictions apply to any part of Teesdale then a visit to the website
www.countrysideaccess.gov.uk will give you all the necessary information.

With using the right to roam and moving away from the recognised footpaths and bridleways, the walker does become more exposed to potential hazards. As with most parts of the North Pennines, Teesdale has in the past been heavily exploited for its mineral wealth. This has left a legacy of old workings, quarries and shafts, all of which can be hazardous. Caution must always be exercised when in the vicinity of any of these sites.

3. The Walks

The nine walks in this book have all been designed to explore the woods, hills and moors surrounding the valley of Teesdale while showcasing the landscape and history of this part of the North Pennines. The walks start from a number of different locations around the length of the valley and illustrate the wide variety of landscapes both within and around this spectacular northern dale. The map on page 9 shows the starting point of each of the walks.

Anybody who has used one of my books before will realise that I have a little bit of a passion for history and how this is reflected in the landscape. As always this is shown within these walks as I quite frequently use them to visit and explore certain aspects of the countryside that I, personally, find quite interesting. I don't believe that walking guidebooks should be boring and, hopefully, the walks and associated notes will help convey my enthusiasm for the landscape of the North Pennines to you, both as a reader and as a walker.

In the details preceding each of the walks there is an approximate time taken for that particular walk which includes a reasonable time to explore the various sites of interest that are visited. However, this can be variable depending upon how long you, as the walker, take to explore these sites. If you chose not to have a look and investigate then the time taken will obviously be shorter whereas if you linger and have a good mooch about then you may be longer than I have estimated. With the huge impact that lead mining had on the dale, it is perhaps inevitable that a number of these walks pass old lead mines and workings and with some of the routes these are actually a feature of the walk. However, resist any temptation to enter and explore these openings as it is extremely dangerous to do so. It is over one hundred years since these mines were abandoned and during the intervening period there has been no maintenance work carried out in them with the result that both rot and erosion has taken it's toll and many of these levels are no longer stable.

The walks in this book have all been graded in accordance with the Ferguson Grading System (`FGS`) and the actual grading is set out at the beginning of each individual walk to help you assess their difficulty. A detailed explanation of the FGS and how individual gradings are determined is set out on pages 111-113 in the Appendix to this book.

4. The Weather

Teesdale itself, covers a wide expanse of land ranging from the high moorland hills of the Pennine range to the less elevated valley floor of the lower dale. In terms of bad weather, when it hits the dale, it can hit it hard. Obviously the higher the altitude and the more exposed the terrain then the greater the effect. The high, moorland hills of the top of the dale can be a joy to walk in the summer but even at this time of year, the weather can be fickle and sudden localised squalls are not uncommon plus snow can often linger quite late into the spring. Even the lower moors that straddle the sides of the dale as it heads eastwards can be exposed if poor weather suddenly comes blowing in. It is always advisable to be fully equipped for all weather conditions when walking in this dale although in the summer months you'll probably be able to do without the heavyweight waterproof and carry a lighter version.

One last bit of advice, a couple of these walks do cross small streams. During and just after heavy rain these may be a little tricky to cross especially as the water levels in the smaller streams coming of the hills can rise quite quickly. In these conditions it may be advisable to chose your walk with a little bit of care.

5. The Maps

Unfortunately more than one map is required to cover the whole of Teesdale. The three maps required are listed below and the relevant map that is needed for each of the walks is shown within the walk instructions.

Ordinance Survey Explorer OL31 North Pennines - Teesdale and Weardale.
Ordinance Survey Explorer OL30 Yorkshire Dales North and Central.
Ordinance Survey Explorer OL19 Howgill Fells & Upper Eden Valley.

The route descriptions included in this book are meant as a guide and although under normal conditions they should be sufficient to guide you round the route they are not intended to replace the use of the relevant map. Nor is the sketch diagram of the route meant to replace the OS map but rather to be used as an aid for you to identify the route on the map.

This countryside can be wild and rough, which is part of it's attraction, and the weather can be very changeable. It is quite possible to set off in brilliant sunshine and then to find that later, low cloud and rain has come rolling in and visibility is very poor. The ability to navigate with map and compass is a required skill to safely traverse these hills and it would be extremely foolhardy to venture out with just this guidebook and no map.

6. Villages, refreshments, accommodation, visitor centres and websites.

As you'll gather from the walks in this book, Teesdale is populated with a number of picturesque little villages, the majority of which have a pub that offers food and drink and in some cases they may have more than one. In addition to this, both Barnard Castle and Middleton-in-Teesdale have a range of cafes and tea rooms to slake your thirst after a walk.

Virtually all of these villages can also provide accommodation ranging from hotels, self-catering to bed and breakfast establishments plus there are a number of camping and caravan sites scattered throughout the dale. Further information on accommodation can be obtained from any of the tourist information centres below.

Within the dale there is the one outdoor shop, 54 Degrees North, which is situated in Barnard Castle. Full details are below:
54 Degrees North, 9 Galgate, Barnard Castle, Co Durham, DL12 8EQ
Telephone 01833 631934 Website www.54degrees-north.co.uk

In terms of tourist information centres and visitor centres, the dale is quite well served with three centres along the length of the dale. From west to east these are:

Bowlees.

The North Pennines Area of Outstanding Natural Beauty have a recently refurbished visitor centre at Bowlees at the western end of the dale. These premises also include a cafe, a gallery, retail outlet, picnic area and quite a large car park.
Bowlees Visitor Centre, Newbiggin,
Barnard Castle, County Durham, DL12 OXF.
Telephone. 01833 528801
Email. info@northpenninesaonb.org.uk

Middleton-in-Teesdale.

Within Middleton-in-Teesdale there is a volunteer-run tourist information centre that operates seven days a week throughout the year between the hours of 10 am and 1 pm.
Middleton in Teesdale Tourist Information Centre, 10 Market Place,
Middleton-in-Teesdale, County Durham, DL12 0QG
Telephone. 01833 641001

Barnard Castle.

The visitor centre in Barnard Castle has recently moved into new premises at the recently re-furbished Witham, a cultural and community centre based in the centre of the town's main street.
The Witham, 3 Horsemarket, Barnard Castle, County Durham, DL12 8LY.
Telephone. 01833 262626.

As well as these visitor centres, Durham County Council operate the official county tourism website at **www.thisisdurham.com**

In addition to the TIC's, there are also a number of websites that give information on the dale in general. Have a look at the following:
www.teesdale.gov.uk
www.teesdalediscovery.com
www.teesdaleholidays.co.uk
www.teesdale.co.uk

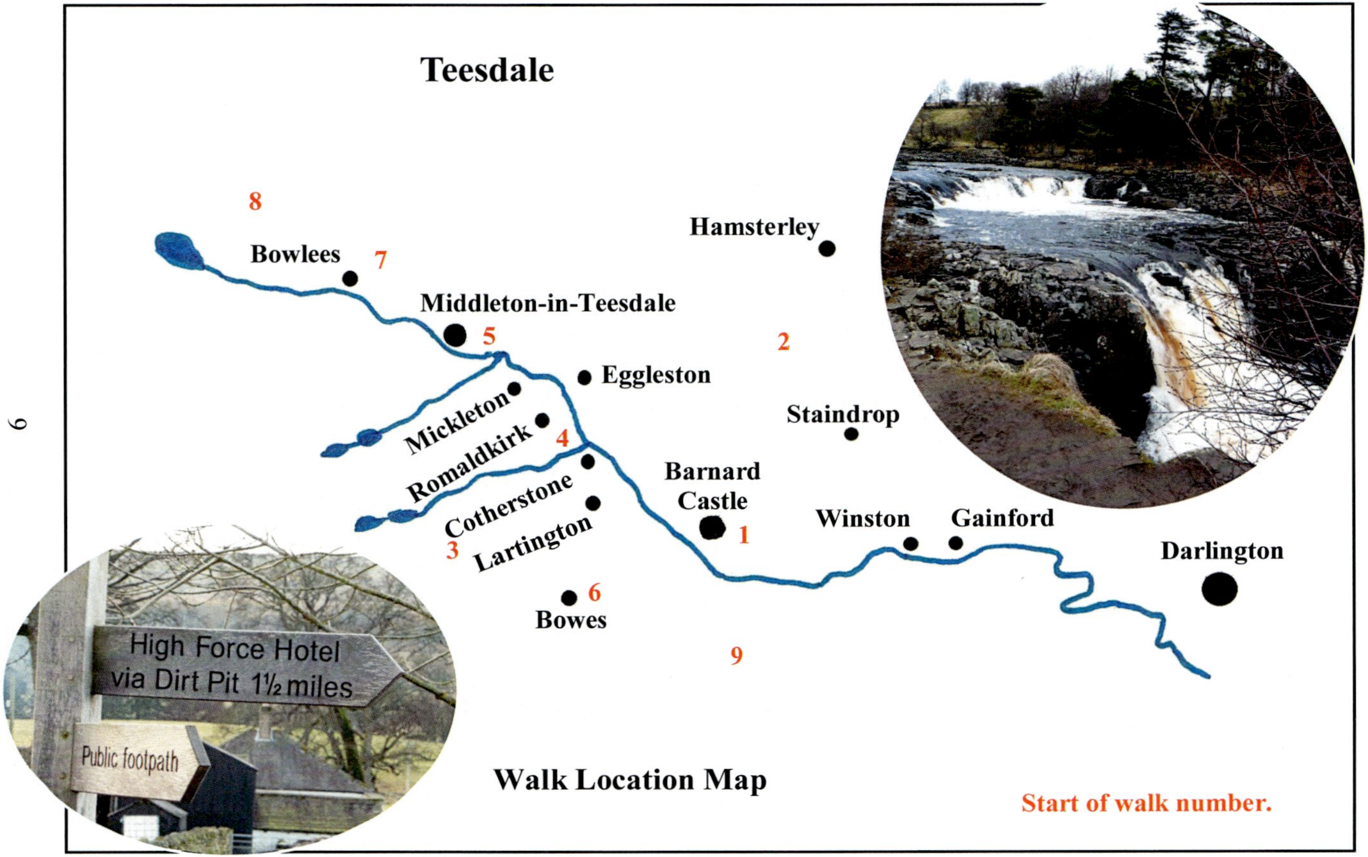

Teesdale
8
Bowlees
7
Middleton-in-Teesdale
5
Eggleston
Mickleton
Romaldkirk
4
Cotherstone
Lartington
3
6
Bowes
Hamsterley
2
Staindrop
Barnard
Castle
1
Winston
Gainford
Darlington
9
High Force Hotel
via Dirt Pit 1½ miles
Public footpath
Walk Location Map
Start of walk number.

The ruins of Egglestone Abbey.
Walk 1. Eggleston Abbey and Boldron.

EGGLESTONE ABBEY

The Abbey of St Mary and St John the Baptist was founded at Eggleston between 1195 and 1198 for the Premonstratensain canons. This was an order of monks founded by St Norbert in 1121 at Premontre in France. They adopted the rules of St Augustine while at the same time also borrowed from the much stricter Cistercians. They were known as the 'White Canons' because of the white habits that they wore. Unlike the monks of the other religious orders they did not follow the practice of isolating themselves from the outside world and undertook preaching and pastoral work throughout the area such as the distribution of food and drink to the needy.

The site at Egglestone was chosen because of it's isolation, it's close proximity to a river and also the supply of local stone for it's construction. The founding of the Abbey was sponsored by the de Moulton family, whose title passed to the Dacres by marriage in 1314. However, the endowment placed upon Egglestone at it's founding was so small that it was impoverished throughout its existence. Because of this lack of funds, early in the 13th century the Abbot of Prémontré sent three of his English abbots to hold an inquiry and decide whether the status of the abbey should be reduced to that of a priory. It remained an abbey, but also remained poor, a condition not helped by it's location in what were then the border lands. The abbey suffered particularly badly when the Scots ravaged Yorkshire in 1315 and then it also suffered under it's own English army who were billeted there in 1346 on their way to the Battle of Neville's Cross near Durham.

The abbey was dissolved by Henry VIII in 1540 and in 1548 it was granted to Robert Strelley who began it's conversion into a private house by converting the east and north ranges into a mansion and installed a kitchen in the west range. During this process the church tower was demolished because it spoilt the view from what was now a manor house. After a series of owners, in 1770 Sir Thomas Robinson sold the abbey to John Morritt of nearby Rokeby Hall. The house was eventually abandoned in the mid-19th century with most of the Abbey being finally pulled down, some of the stonework being used to pave the stable yard at Rokeby Hall during the 19th century. The descendants of John Morritt finally placed the ruins of the Abbey in the guardianship of the state in 1925 and later returned a notable collection of architectural stonework, including the tomb of Sir Ralph Bowes of Streatlam, who died in 1482, and this was re-erected in the church crossing.

The buildings on the site have been declared a Scheduled Ancient Monument and are being maintained by English Heritage. Admission to the site is free.

WALK 1: EGGLESTONE ABBEY AND BOLDRON

The first walk in the book traverses the countryside to the south of the River Tees, between Barnard Castle and the A66 Trans-Pennine route. Formerly part of Yorkshire before the local government reorganisation of the 1970's, this part of the dale is not often walked which is a bit of a shame really as it is an area that has it's own attractions. Along the way you'll pass the ruins of the most northern of the monastic houses of Yorkshire. Although a lesser cousin of the great abbeys of Rievaulx, Jervaulx and Fountains, the remains of Egglestone Abbey are still quite spectacular albeit on a smaller scale. From the abbey the route makes it's way up to the small village of Boldron, a village that through it's old well, may have a link to one of the greatest kings of England, Athelstan, grandson of Alfred the Great and the first king to unite all of the country that became England and indeed, the first king to have dominance over the whole of the British Isles.

DISTANCE: 5.4 miles / 8.6 km.
ASCENT: 574 feet / 175 metres.
TERRAIN: Mainly field paths and tracks with a couple of short stretches of road walking along quiet country lanes. Although there is some climbing on this walk there is nothing that can be considered significant.
TIME: 3½ to 4 hours.
START: The Butter Market in Barnard Castle. GR NZ 050 163. There is ample parking within Barnard Castle that gives access to the Butter Market.
MAP: OL31:North Pennines. Teesdale and Weardale.
ACCESS: The route is all on public rights of way.
DOGS: As the route is all on public rights of way then dogs are allowed. However, be aware that the route does go through the middle of a caravan park and that you will also encounter both sheep and cattle throughout this route so please keep your dog under close control preferably on a lead.

GRID REFERENCES

Butter Market	050 163
Path/road junction	061 153
Entrance road	063 151
Path/road junction	050 140
Boldron	037 143
Footbridge	039 149
Butter Market	050 163

The Butter Market and, inset, the view downstream from the footbridge over the Tees.

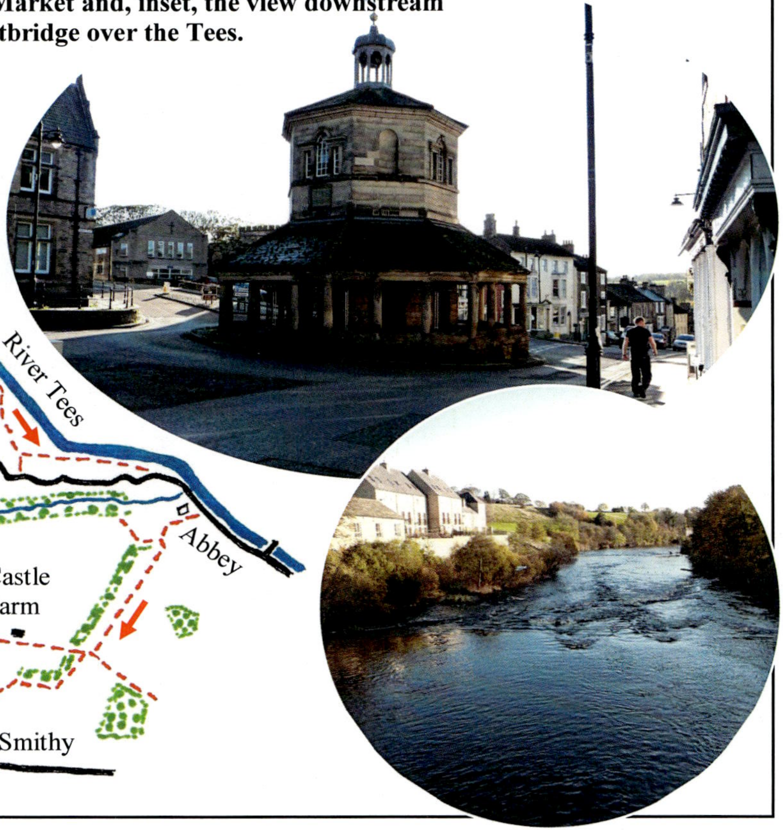

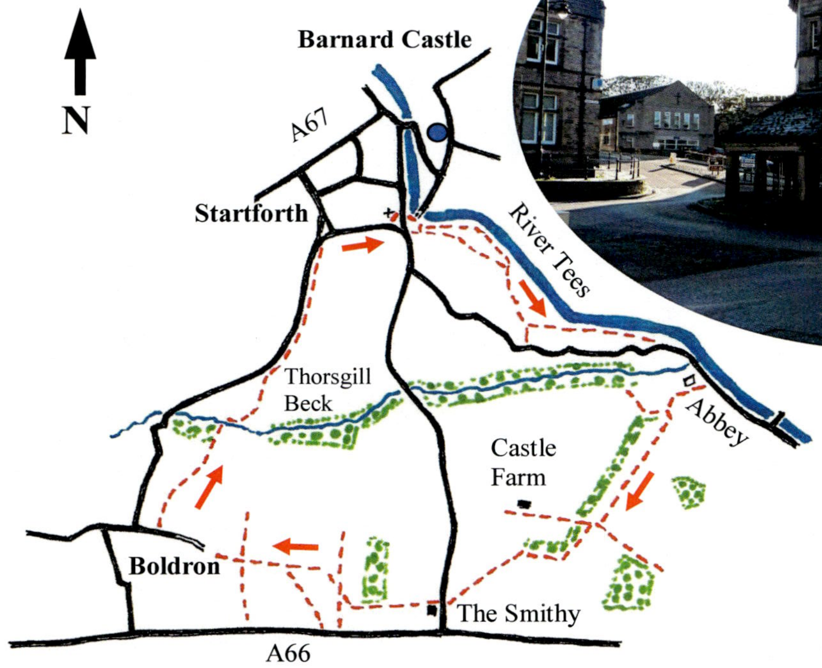

FGS GRADING

Grading is T4 [D0, N1, T1, R1, H1]

Distance	**0**	Up to 6 miles
Navigation	**1**	Basic navigation skills needed
Terrain	**1**	50 – 75% on graded track or path, 25 – 50% off track
Remote-ness	**1**	Countryside in fairly close proximity to habitation – at least 80% of the route within 2 miles
Height	**1**	Over 100 ft per mile

THE WALK

1. From the Butter Market head down the bank and where the main road turns right continue straight on to cross a footbridge over the river Tees. Once across turn left to follow the riverside path as indicated by the marker post "Public Footpath to Egglestone Abbey". The path leads you past a string of houses on the right and at one point you come to a junction with another path going off on the right but just continue straight on alongside the river.

Passing a small weir on the River Tees.

After a while you'll pass the last of the houses and shortly after that the path bears right to leave the river and enter a caravan park. Turn left onto the tarmac drive and follow it for a short distance to a visible marker post. Here turn right to head uphill following the signs to the exit, stay on the drive as it bears left to come to another marker post and an exit sign. Turn right to follow the signs and leave the caravans behind and come to an open grassed area. As you approach the white goal posts on the right, there is a waymarked stile on the left next to a red dog waste bin. Cross the stile and go over the brow of the low hill in front to come to a gateway. Go through and follow the hedge and fence on the left over the next three fields to come to a stile leading onto the roadside. **GR 061 153.**

2. Turn left to follow the road as it descends down to run alongside the Tees. After a short distance the road crosses a bridge over the Thorsgill Beck and here on the right side of the bridge lies an old packhorse bridge.

Called the Bow Bridge, this old packhorse bridge was built at some point in the 1600's to cross the Thorsgill beck. It is a typical hog-backed bridge with a single arch and low parapets. The surface of the bridge is still paved with large cobbles. A well-trodden path runs over the bridge where walker's inquisitiveness compel them to try the bridge.

Continue along the road for a short distance to come to the entrance road to Eglestone Abbey. **GR 063 151.**

3. Turn right to head up to the Abbey which as you are passing is well-worth a small detour to have a look around. When you've left the Abbey continue along the access road, ignoring the footpath sign at the edge of the car park, towards Abbey Farm.

Heading towards Abbey Farm.

Before you get to the farm take the first turning on the left, there is a public bridleway sign at this corner but it is obscured by a hedge and quite difficult to see. Follow the track past the last building and go through the gate in front to come to a junction with a marker post set right back against the hedge. Turn left to go through another gate and once through, turn right to follow the left side of both the hedge and stream, up a slight climb to come to a gate complete with footpath marker.

Go through and continue straight ahead following the right side of the field to come to another gate and marker. Again, go through and continue straight ahead to come to the end of the field and here turn right to cross a stream and head towards the line of trees. However, just before you reach the trees you'll come to a gate on the left with a footpath marker on it. Go through the gate and cross the sleeper bridge and, ignoring the track on the right that goes between the trees, continue straight ahead following the left side of the trees round the outside of the field. When you reach the end of the trees you'll come to a very wonky stile in the fence on the right next to a metal water tank. Turn right to cross the stile and follow the left side of the wood to a gateway with a footpath marker.

Following the direction of the marker, head diagonally across the field making for where the line of the hedge in the field beyond can be seen joining the bottom fence and here come to a broken down stile on the left side of a bush. Take care going over both the stile and the ditch on the other side, and then bear right through a gap into the next field. Head diagonally left across this field making for a group of trees that seem marginally taller than the others, to come to another broken stile next to a large boulder.

Cross and go across the narrow strip of trees to join the roadside opposite The Smithy. **GR 050 140.**

4. Cross the road and go through the gate on the right of the buildings as indicated by the marker post and follow the track as it bends to the right behind the farm and follows a hedge on the left. Continue into the second field where the track disappears and the hedge on the left now becomes a fence. As you approach the tree line at the end of the field you'll come to a double-stile in the fence on the left. Cross and turn right to continue following the fence only now on the left side of it. When you get to the end of the trees you'll come to another stile to cross back over the fence but once you have, don't continue following the fence, instead head diagonally across the field towards a stile about half-way between the two large oak trees.

Once there, cross and following the direction of the marker arrow, head diagonally right to a gate on the opposite side of the field. Go through the gate and again following the marker arrow go straight ahead to the now visible houses of Boldron.

The OS map shows you crossing a number of narrow strip fields although in reality the majority of the hedgerows dividing the fields have disappeared leaving single large fields. These long "strip" fields are an indicator of Medieval farming practices as are the undulations encountered in many of the fields, a practice known as Rigg and Furrow.

When you get to the other side of the field you'll come to a double-stile and marker. Cross and go straight ahead through a gap in an old hedge and then bear to the left of the building in front to pick up a track on the other side which will lead you to a gate to enter the village. **GR 037 143.**

Boldron is an old village, being referred to as "Bulerun" in 1280 meaning "Bull clearing". As you'll notice the village is out of the way, which is one of it's main attractions.

5. Continue through the village passing a footpath sign on the right and a short distance after, as you pass Fair View Cottage but before you get to the picnic tables, turn right to go down the footpath in front of Woodbine Cottage that leads to a wall stile. There is a metal footpath sign next to the cottage but this is not immediately visible from the roadside, at least not until you pass it. Go over the stile and the second stile beyond it and go straight across the following field to a stile on the opposite side.

As you follow this section of the walk you'll notice that there has been a great deal of renovation work performed on the path and in particular on the stone steps leading to the field stiles. This has all been part of a community project led by Boldron parish history group and which includes a two-mile walk, part of which route you are now following.

Cross the stile and following the direction of the marker arrow, bear diagonally right to another stile in the field corner. Once over, continue heading in the same direction to another stile on the opposite side of the field and then go straight over the next field making for a stile to the left of the field barn. Cross into the next field and head down to the stone structure in the middle of the field. Renovated in 2007 under the project led by the History group, this is Boldron Well.

BOLDRON WELL

Boldron Well, which is also known as Athelstan's Well, lies a short distance north of the village and is significant as being the only village well that never runs dry. The current structure, which was rebuilt in 2007, dates from around 1879 although the well has existed for a long time before that. The earliest written record is in a 1768 Act of Parliament for the Enclosure of Boldron Moor in which the well was named.

How the well gained it's name Athelstan's Well is a mystery. There are two theories, the first being that Athelstan, the grandson of Alfred the Great and the first king to unite all of England, passed this way in 927 while on the march to subdue King Constantine of Scotland and the northern kings after he had taken York from the Danes. The second theory, and the more likely, is that Athelstan is a corruption of Egglestone. The abbey is only 1500 metres east of the well and even now, water is piped from the well to troughs in the fields next to the ruins. When the abbey was at it's height there may have been similar connections with the well providing water for the monks.

From the well continue heading downhill on the right side of the field to come to Thorsgill Beck and make a second crossing of the stream, this time on an old stone footbridge. **GR 039 149.**

Known as Paddock Bridge, this small, narrow, stone bridge is an old pack-horse bridge and has crossed Thorsgill Beck from at least the 1700's. The low parapets on either side of the bridge were deliberately low to give sufficient room for the panniers strapped on both sides of the horse to pass over the walls.

6. Once over the bridge turn right to follow the beck downstream for 20 metres to cross the fence into the next field and here, following the marker arrow, go diagonally left up the slight slope of the hill to come to a gate complete with stile and direction marker. At this point there are some stunning views over Barnard Castle and the Tees valley with the Bowes Museum being very prominent.

Cross the stile and, keeping the hedge on the left, head downhill to approach a gateway leading on to the road. Don't go through the gate but instead stay within the field to go over the stile in front that lies in the gap between the trees, to follow a path with the roadside hedge on the left and a small, relatively new plantation on the right. When you come to the end of the trees continue on following the hedge on the left, which has become a wall for a short distance before reverting back to a hedge. Ignore the gate and footpath marker post that you'll pass on the left to continue by the edge of the field.

When you get to the buildings of Startforth Hall Farm go through the gate on the left to continue down through the field next to the road and when you get to the bottom, go through a squeeze stile to exit onto the road. Now bear right to follow the side road round the outside of the wall and then go past the next junction on the left to pass the Morritt Memorial Schools, taking the opportunity cross the road and walk down the pavement on the left side. Stay on the path to come to the Church of the Holy Trinity.

The Church of the Holy Trinity and, inset, the lych gate of the church

This beautiful little church was built in 1863 to replace an earlier Medieval one. A glance in the churchyard shows that some of the gravestones easily pre-date the building of the church. Set within the porch are six 13th century carved slabs presumably from the original building.

Continue past the church and turn left through the gate at the footpath marker post to descend down through Church Bank Field, which has now been replanted as a garden area for the village. At the bottom of the field come to the side of the road and bear right to the riverside path that will take you back to the now visible footbridge over the Tees that you used at the start of the walk. Cross the bridge and head back up the bank, back to the Butter Market.

The Steel Road.
Walk 2. Arn Gill.

THE MINES OF ARN GILL AND COWLEY

The Durham coalfield had been worked for centuries albeit not on a large industrial scale, that didn't begin until the 1800's. However, most people don't realise that the southern edge of this coalfield reached down to the northern borders of Teesdale.

By 1857, the villages of Woodland, Copley and Cockfield, an area on the northern side of Teesdale known as the Upper Gaunless Valley, boasted a total of 549 collieries, drifts and shafts. Most of these being small privately owned concerns employing only small numbers of men. Between 1892 and 1894 trial boring was carried out west of Copley to estimate the extent of the coal reserves here. Sufficient reserves were proved and from 1894 to 1896 two shafts were sunk at what was to become Cowley Colliery.

The extracted coal was moved from Cowley to the Woodland (Back) Pit by tramway. At the Woodland Pit the coal was then loaded onto a spur of the Bishop Auckland to Barnard Castle Railway. A tramway was a narrow guage rail line where the wagons, or tubs as they were called, were attached to cables and hauled by stationery steam engines. The Woodland Pit actually stood on the other side of Woodland village to Cowley and so the tramway ran up to and then underneath the village through a specially constructed tunnel.

By 1905 the coal reserves in the small valley of Arn Gill were being worked and the Woodland tramway was extended by nearly two miles to run into the Gill. Over the next forty years, three drift mines were opened in the valley, Arngill Middle and Western Drifts, and the Duke of York Drift then, in 1947, the Arnghyll Drift Mine was opened by the newly created National Coal Board which combined all the existing drifts in the valley.

However, coal reserves do become exhausted and in 1921 the Woodland Pit closed down. Despite the closure of this pit, the haulage engine continued in operation pulling the coal along the tramways from Arn Gill for loading on to the railway spur on the other side of the village. The engine was finally shut down two years later in 1923. By then an aerial ropeway had been installed linking Arn Gill to the Gibbsnees siding, again on the Bishop Auckland to Barnard Castle Railway.

In 1951 the Arnghyll Drift was closed due to the threat of flooding from the old Woodland Pit workings. Within two years the site had been totally cleared including the old steam haulage engine, the tramways and the aerial ropeway complete with carrying towers and storage hoppers. Trees have now been planted to hide the scars of Arn Gill's mining era but in the upper reaches of this small valley the graded routes of the old tramways can still be seen along the valley floor.

WALK 2: ARN GILL.

To the north of Teesdale lie a number of small springs and streams that form hanging valleys that run above the northern slopes of the main dale. Some of these watercourses run down to join the Tees while others join to form the River Gaunless which runs north-east to ultimately join the River Wear

This is an area that is not often walked, which is a bit of a shame really as it is a part of Teesdale that is full of surprises not least the fact that it is more closely associated with the coal mines of central Durham rather than the lead mines of the upper dale.

DISTANCE: 7.1 miles / 11.3 km.
ASCENT: 833 feet / 254 metres.
TERRAIN: The majority of this walk is on field paths over pasture land, however, some of this is rough pasture with an uneven surface that will probably have been churned up by livestock. At the beginning and the end of the walk, the route follows tracks through woodland. There is one short, steep climb as you come out of Arn Gill.
TIME: 4½ to 5 hours.
START: Small road-side car park at the Copley Smelt Mill which lies on the Barnard Castle - Copley and Woodland road. GR NZ 086 250.
MAP: OL31. North Pennines. Teesdale and Weardale.
ACCESS: The route is all on public rights of way.
DOGS: As the route is all on rights of way then dogs are allowed, however, please keep them under close control, preferably on a lead. The majority of the walk crosses pasture land and so livestock will be encountered in most of the fields. During spring many of the fields do contain young lambs. There are a number of high stiles that your dog may need to be lifted over.

GRID REFERENCES

Parking space	086 250
Gate and stile	076 255
Cowley Colliery	068 253
Gate and stile	064 254
Track/road junction	064 245
Road/track junction	055 245
Bridge	054 238
East House Cottage	054 232
Beckside	060 226

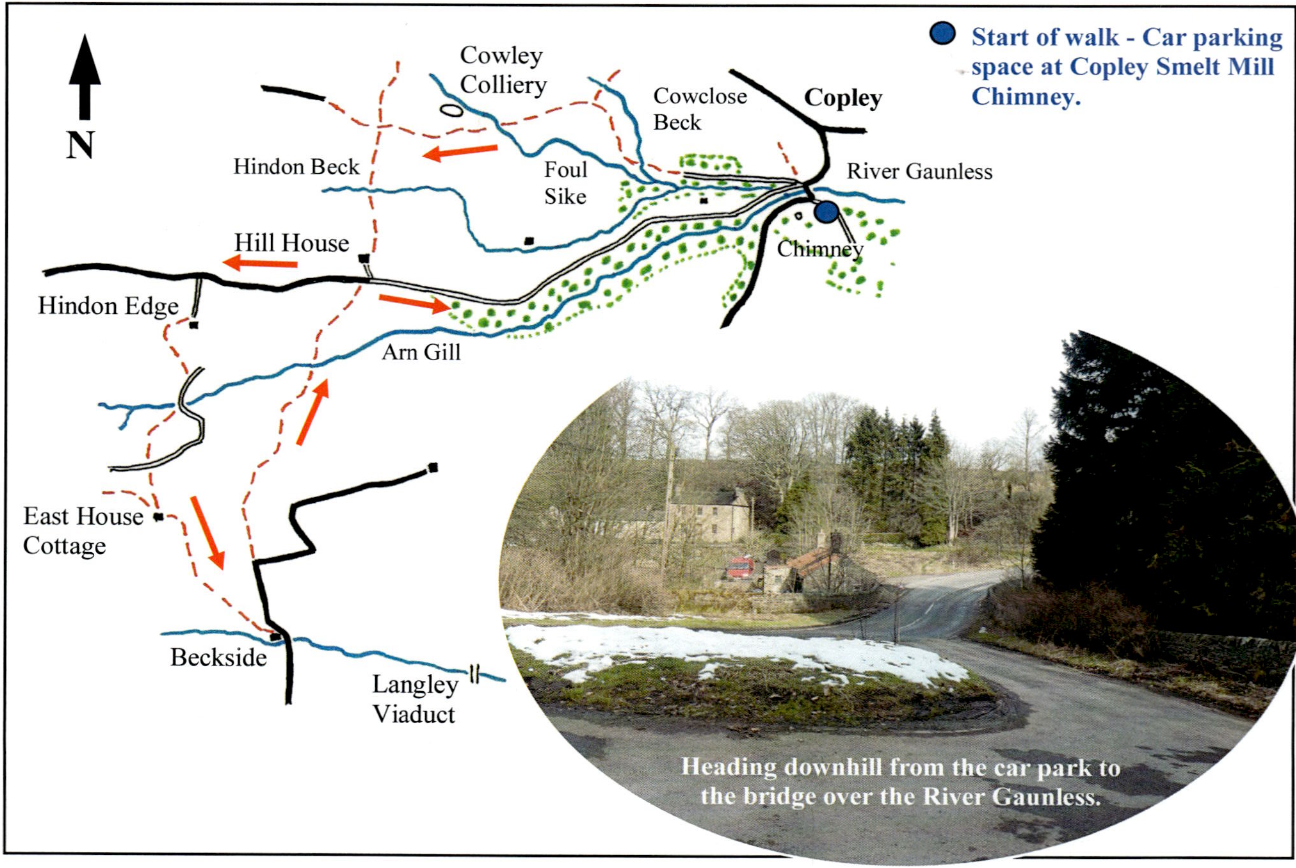

Heading downhill from the car park to the bridge over the River Gaunless.

Road/path junction	058 230
Path/road junction	063 245
Parking space	086 250

FGS GRADING

Grading is T5 [D1, N1, T1, R1, H1]

Distance	**1**	6 – 12 miles
Navigation	**1**	Basic navigation skills needed
Terrain	**1**	50 – 75% on graded track or path, 25 – 50% off track
Remote-ness	**1**	Countryside in fairly close proximity to habitation – at least 80% of the route within 2 miles
Height	**1**	Over 100 ft per mile

THE WALK

1. From the car park, head downhill to cross the bridge over the River Gaunless and follow the road a short way up the other side to come to a track on the left with a footpath marker post pointing up it. Turn left to leave the road here but instead of following the main track, turn right up a second track that joins it and which has a bridleway marker post pointing up it.

The second track with the bridleway marker.

Follow this new track as it heads uphill, ignoring the steps that go off to the right shortly after starting it. After a little while the track enters Cowclose Plantation and after passing through, exits into a field. Here follow the right-hand fence to come to a red gate with a stile next to it.

Cross the stile and continue to follow the fence, now with it on your left, to come to a small gate that leads on to a little bridge over the Cowclose Beck. Cross the bridge and bear left to a waymarked post and then, from this post, turn right to follow the obvious track as it heads slightly uphill to exit the trees.

As you come out of the trees, bear slightly to the right to make for a waymarked gate standing in the field, the gate is a little isolated, having no fence or wall connected to either end. Following the marker on the gate, go straight ahead over the rise and once over the top, bear left to a visible gate and stile where the fence and wall on that side meet. **GR 076 255.**

2. Cross the stile and follow the track that is on the other side as it goes straight ahead to the next gate and stile. Cross and then the first sign of the area's mining past appears on the right, an old colliery waste heap.

The old colliery waste heap.

Continue to follow the track to the next gate and stile and cross. The track now goes over a small rise and starts to descend down to a patch of gorse bushes, passing a marker post on the way.

The slight descent gives the first viewing of the industrial complex that was the Cowley Colliery. Over to the right stand two very large waste tips and between runs an old tramway which heads towards you before turning to the left to cross your path and then head over towards a distant Arn Gill.

A distant view of Cowley Colliery with the tramways in evidence.

Go through the gorse bushes to come to a small gate and then a wooden bridge over the Foul Sike. A tellingly-named stream which presumably got it's name because it originated near the mine workings.

Continue following the track ahead but now with a fence on your left. As you get closer to the heaps, the fence turns off to the left but continue on the track and as you pass the spoil heaps you'll come to what was an old information board, standing on the right of the track. Now bare, the board used to give details of what could be seen of the old workings from this spot. **GR 068 253.**

The bare information board next to the brick lining of one of the two shafts at the colliery, now filled in and, inset, the concrete base of the steam engine that provided the power for the colliery.

3. Continue along the track to the next gate and stile and cross. When in this field, over to the right the undulating ground gives evidence of a medieval rigg and furrow ploughing system. Continue on to the next gate and stile, which is waymarked. **GR 064 254.**

Evidence of medieval rigg and furrow ploughing.

4. Cross the stile but ignore the track that goes straight ahead and instead turn left to follow another track as it goes over a low ridge to two standing gate posts. Many of the older maps show Cowley Farm standing here, this is no longer the case, just the odd piece of brick and concrete remain. Go between the gateposts and continue straight ahead downhill, making for a small gate in the bottom wall of the field, ignore the larger gate over on the left. When you get there, go through and descend to the footbridge that crosses the Hindon Beck.

Cross the bridge and, following the waymarker on it, continue straight ahead, uphill to a visible stile on the skyline. When you get to the top of the bank, cross the stile and then make for the buildings of Hill House. As you approach the farm, head to the left-hand gate which has a stile next to it and cross into the yard. Follow the yard round to the left of the buildings to join the farm's access track and then follow this track down to the side of a road. **GR 064 245.**

5. Turn right to follow the road for 800 metres until you come to a track on the left that goes to the farm of Hindon Edge. A footpath marker post points up the track. **GR 055 245.**

6. Turn left to leave the road and follow the track down to the farm. As you approach the buildings, you'll come to a marker post that directs you right, off the well-made track and on to a rougher one that takes you past the front of the buildings. This track takes you past another marker post and also past a gate at the end of the buildings and then continues following the wall on the left to come to a second gate, this one waymarked.

Go through the gate and continue straight ahead downhill, following the wall on the left. When the wall ends at a corner, continue straight ahead to go over the edge of the valley and come to a track. Bear right to follow the track down into the valley and to a small bridge that crosses the Arn Gill. **GR 054 238.**

Looking down into the Arn Gill valley and one of the old tramways now used as a farm track and, inset, following the track down into the valley.

7. Cross the bridge and here leave the track as it bends to the left and you bear slightly to the right to follow a quad bike track steeply up the side of the hill. When you get to the top of the ridge, you'll see that it drops quite steeply down to a marshy area, turn right to follow the ridge for a couple of hundred metres until it meets a track. Here turn left to follow the track down to a gate in the wall opposite.

Go through the gate and follow the now faint track straight ahead, crossing over another more substantial track, and making for the right-hand gate in front.

Once through this, head down to the left-side of East House Cottage which can be seen in front. **GR 054 232.**

The descent down across the field gives an early view of the Langley Viaduct, which can be seen over on the left, which was part of the old Bishop Auckland to Barnard Castle railway.

8. When you are stood next to the cottage, ignore the gate straight in front and bear left to the bottom left-hand corner of the field to come to a waymarked gate. Go through and follow the left-hand hedge down to another gate. Once through this, continue to follow the left-hand wall part-way down the field until you come to a waymarked gate set into it.

Go through and now head diagonally left, down and across the field making for a gateway half-way down the opposite side. As a marker, the white painted farm of Beckside lies in the distance behind the gateway, head towards the farm and you'll come to the gate.

Go through the gateway and then cut the corner of the next field, making for a stile over the fence, just to the right of where the farm appears in the distance. Once over this, make straight for the farm, passing to the right of an isolated barn, to come to a stile next to the main buildings which leads onto a road. **GR 060 226.**

9. Ignore the footpath sign on the opposite side of the road and turn left to follow the road uphill until you come to where it turns sharply right and here you'll find a footpath marker post pointing straight ahead. **GR 058 230.**

10. Leave the road at this corner and go straight ahead following the fence and hedge on the left and going past a gate in the hedge. When you get to the field corner, go through the gate and continue to follow the left-hand fence and hedge for about 200 metres and then bear right to head over to the fence next to the trees. There is no immediately visible way over the wire fence, however, a rough stile made up of large stones either side of the fence is easy to cross.

Once over, head diagonally right across the next field, going slightly uphill over a rise. You are making for a stone stile that is built into the opposite wall but because of what it is, this is difficult to see until you are more or less on top of it and you may have to look up and down the wall to find it.

Climb over the stile and then go straight over the next field making for the way-marked gate a short distance away. Go through and, following the direction shown by the waymarker, go over the rise and then head to the left of the wall corner to come to a gate.

Once through the gate, you'll pick up a rough track that heads down into Arn Gill to cross the gill by a small bridge downstream from the ponds. As you descend, the route up the other side of the valley is clearly visible and you will be heading for Hill House Farm on the opposite bank.

Descending into Arn Gill.

From the bridge on the valley floor, bear diagonally right up to the visible wall corner where you will find a stone stile to take you over the wall, again this is a little difficult to see until you are on top of it. Once across the stile, head directly uphill towards the farm buildings, crossing a shallow gully on the way. Just before you get to the buildings, you'll reach the side of a road. **GR 063 245.**

11. The farm in front is Hill House, which no doubt you recognise from the outward leg of the walk. Turn right to follow the road past the entrance track to the farm and then cross the cattle grid to continue straight ahead along the track that runs above the edge of the valley.

This track is known as the Steele Road and is the route that linked Eggleston with the smelt mill at Copley. It was along this road that the ore payable to the Raby Estate was transported to be smelted. The name of the road coming from the silver/grey colour of the track due to the dropped lead ore.

Follow the track as it soon starts to run along the top of a plantation. The trees have been planted since the 1950's to mask what remains of the industrial scars caused by the mining in Arn Gill. Close inspection still reveals remains of concrete and brick at the side of the track.

The route from here is fairly straight forward, just following the track for the next 2 km as it descends down into the valley. Along the way you'll pass the entrances to Burfoot Leazes and, after a lengthy while, Steele House, both of them on the left.

As you near the end of the track and approach the houses on the valley floor, you'll cross a bridge over the Cowclose Beck, which goes on behind the house on the right to join the Arn Gill and form the River Gaunless. As you go between the houses, take the upper track which takes you past the old mill manager's house, on the left, to join the side of the road. Here turn right to go back over the bridge crossing the Gaunless and up to the parking space.

Copley Smelt Mill

During the heyday of lead mining in Teesdale, during the 1700 and 1800's, the vast bulk of the land on the north side of the river was owned, as it still is, by the Raby Estate. The rights to mine for minerals under the ground were let to various mining companies for a financial consideration which was generally paid as a proportion of the ore extracted and was quite literally handed over as a quantity of ore.

This ore then had to be smelted in order to produce the valuable lead which could then be sold. So around 1770 to 1790, the 3rd Earl of Darlington, the head of the family owning the estate, had a smelt mill built on the banks of the River Gaunless. The location of the mill may seem a bit strange at first as it is located a good distance away from the lead mines where the ore was produced. However, the mill was on the southern edge of the Durham coalfield and a number of smaller mines were on Raby Estate land thus making the coal and the heat that it provided within the smelting process relatively cheap. Plus there was also the water power from the river to operate the machinery of the mill.

The mill itself stood on the other side of the bridge, on the north side of the river where the houses now stand. Unfortunately the only original building from the mill still standing is the mill manager's house, now a private dwelling, which is the northern-most building separated from the other buildings by the track. From the mill a conducting flue carried the poisonous fumes from the smelting process across the river and up the hill to a chimney where they were dispersed into the atmosphere. Very little remains of the flue now and it is very difficult to trace it's path from the mill to the chimney. However, the sandstone chimney still stands on top of the hill and is now a listed building.

The mill operated for around a hundred years, up to around 1870 to 1880.

The trig point on Lamb Hill.
Walk 3: The Two Trigs of Baldersdale.

WALK 3: THE TWO TRIGS OF BALDERSDALE

The River Balder is one of the main tributaries of the upland River Tees and together with the Lune, forms what is known as Teesdale's Lakeland due to the number of reservoirs contained within these two small valleys. On the south side of Baldersdale lie a range of low hills that sweep down into Sled Dale and, ultimately, to Stainmore itself.

This walk explores the open moorland on this side of the dale and takes in the two trig points that line this side of the valley. This is a walk of far horizons, as the advertising blurb would say. Despite their relatively low height, these hills give wide ranging views deep into the Pennines and across to the other side of Teesdale. Here you can, quite truthfully, feel as if you were walking across the top of the world.

DISTANCE: 8.8 miles / 14.1 km.
ASCENT: 712 feet / 217 metres.
TERRAIN: Most of this walk is over pathless open moor. This involves rough ground and in many places this also means wet and boggy. On the return leg you follow a moorland track down Race Yate Rigg but it is only in the final stretches from Battle Hill Farm that this becomes dry and solid. There is a short road section on this walk. Although there is a fair amount of climbing there is nothing that is particularly steep, it is more long and gradual.
TIME: 4¼ to 4¾ hours.
START: Car parking space at the end of the minor road that leads to Booze Wood Farm. GR NY 987 189.
MAP: OL31. North Pennines. Teesdale and Weardale.
ACCESS: This route uses a combination of public rights of way and open access land with most of the open moor walking being on the open access land. Even when rights of way are used to cross the moor, these rarely exist on the ground and are easily lost.
DOGS: Not allowed on the access land.

GRID REFERENCES

Parking space	987 189
Gate and stile	968 180
Path junction	964 176
Gate	965 172
West Hare Crag	949 166
Gate and stile	942 161

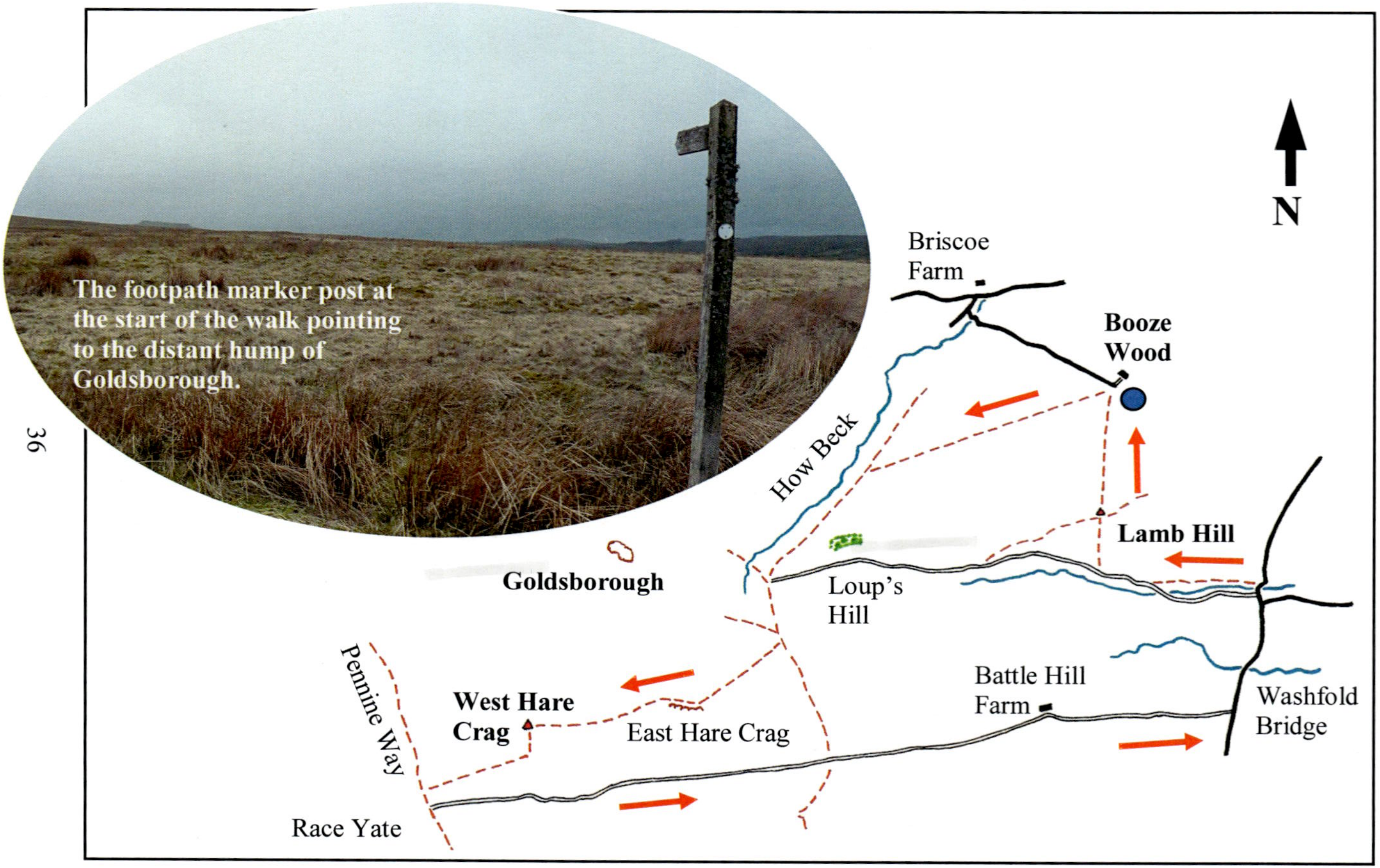

The footpath marker post at the start of the walk pointing to the distant hump of Goldsborough.

Gate	969 164
Track/road junction	994 167
Road/track junction	996 175
Side-stream	988 176
Track bend	985 177
Ruined vehicle	985 179
Lamb Hill	986 180
Parking space	987 189

FGS GRADING
Grading is F6 [D1, N1, T2, R2, H0]

Distance	**1**	6 – 12 miles
Navigation	**1**	Basic navigation skills needed
Terrain	**2**	25 -50% on graded track or path, 50 – 75% off track
Remote-ness	**2**	Countryside not in close proximity to habitation – less than 20% of the route within 2 miles
Height	**0**	Less than 100 ft per mile

THE WALK

1. From the car parking space, follow the footpath sign that stands at the corner of the space and head west across the moor making for the distinctive flat-topped hill of Goldsborough that can be seen in the distance. The route crosses open moor going over a number of low rises with the resulting wet and boggy

Heading towards Goldsborough.

bits in-between but in general the route is slowly climbing to a low ridge. As you progress, over on the left the walls that surround Loup's Hill, with it's clump of trees, become more distinctive.

Continue climbing towards Goldsborough and eventually you'll come to a wire fence running along the side of the deep gully of the How Beck. A faint but distinctive path runs alongside the fence. Turn left to follow this path to a gate and stile that lie only a short distance away. **GR 968 180.**

The side of How Beck.

2. Cross the stile, take a bit of care as it wobbles a bit, and continue to follow the path as it makes it's way between the walls surrounding Loup's Hill on the left and the steep gully on the right. Gradually the path gets closer to the wall until it is running alongside it and then, after a short distance, comes to a gate in the wall and a junction of paths. **GR 964 176.**

3. Ignore the paths that go off either side and continue on the path straight ahead, going between the wall and an old marker post, and heading towards the walls in the near distance. The path bends to the right to approach the wall and then follows it, with the wall on your left, to come to a gate where the Pennine Way passes through it. **GR 965 172.**

4. Don't go through the gate but instead turn right to follow the wall uphill, keeping it on your left. The wall itself soon becomes nothing more than a line of fallen stones in the grass and is replaced by a wire fence. A faint quad bike track now starts to run alongside the fence and this makes the walking just that little bit easier but not much.

After a slow steady climb, you'll start to approach the beginning of East Hare Crag, recognisable by the two large mounds to the left of the fence. Here the ground levels out and you'll find yourself on top of a low range of crags. The left-hand fence has now been replaced by a wall and you'll find that it descends to run round the front of the crag. At this point you're better off not following it but instead make your way along the top of the crag, the crag top gradually descends to meet the wall again anyway and going across the top is far easier walking.

The wall is followed for a short distance but it then starts to descend slightly into a more marshy area where once again it becomes a fence. The trig point on West Hare Crag should now be visible on top of it's low cliffs. If you leave the wall/fence now and make a more direct line for the concrete trig point you'll find that you can follow a slightly higher ridge of ground that does give you, in the main, a bit of a drier walk.

As you progress along the ridge, the trig point does disappear from view for a short while but as you get closer it reappears and you soon get to it. **GR 949 166.**

The trig point on West Hare Crag with Goldsborough in the background.

5. At the trig point, turn left, due south, to descend down the face of the low crag, this is actually a lot easier than it sounds, and follow the faint path that exists over the soft ground to the wall. The wall goes over a small rise at this point and if you head for where it goes over the high point of the rise, you'll find an old boundary stone built into the wall.

Once at the wall, turn right to follow it, keeping it on your left. The wall descends and changes back into a fence as it crosses Brown Rigg Moss on it's way to the next rise. And yes, the crossing of this low area is as wet and boggy as it's name suggests.

As you near this next rise, the ground begins to slope upward and it does become much drier. You'll also see a Pennine Way signpost silhouetted against the sky. When you get to the top of the rise, you'll find a gate and stile next to the sign post. **GR 942 161.**

Approaching the Pennine Way,

6. Turn left to go through the gate and follow the left-hand wall for about 20 metres until you come to a waymarked gate in it. Turn left through the gate onto a green moorland track. This track is now followed as it slowly descends down the ridge with wide views over on the right across the valley of the Deepdale Beck. Although a distinctive track, in places it is still wet and boggy and at times you have to go around a couple of wet bits. Eventually the track arrives at a gate. **GR 969 164.**

7. Go through the gate and continue on the track, which now has more of a hard surface, to Battle Hill Farm which lies in front. When you get to the farm, go through the gate and then bear right and then almost immediately, turn left again to another gate. Go through this to join the access track for the farm and here turn right to follow it away from the farm and through three gateways, the last one leading onto a roadside. **GR 994 167.**

8. Turn left to follow the road downhill to cross the Washfold Bridge and then start climbing up the other side. After going over the top of the climb, the road starts to descend down a slight dip and here you'll pass a road junction on the right. A few metres after this you'll come to a track leaving the left side of the road. This track lies just in front of a cattle grid and a small bridge over the Scur Beck. There is also a footpath marker post pointing through a small pedestrian gate. **GR 996 175.**

The footpath marker post and track at the Scur Beck Bridge.

9. Here you have an option. The footpath goes through the small gate and then follows the left side of the beck. However, this is rough and steep banks along the side of the beck do, in places, block your progress. The alternative is to follow the track. As it first leaves the road, the track has a large sign on it's right side proclaiming that you are now entering an MOD firing range. The range itself is behind the left-hand wall and the track lies just outside it. The track can be followed as it runs above the beck until it descends to cross it and move to the right-hand bank.

If, however, you don't fancy getting that close to the range or the red flags are flying and you just want to be a little bit further away from the bangs, then you can follow the road over the bridge to the other side of the beck and here you'll find a clear path leaving the left-side of the road and following the beck up-stream. After a little while the path leaves the side of the beck and moves to the right, going up the side of the bank and passing the remains of an old tin hut. When you get up to the lip of the small valley, turn to the left to continue heading upstream albeit above the beck below. It's not long before you come to the point where the track crosses the beck and you can make the short descent to join it.

From the point where the track crosses the beck, continue to follow the track as it moves a little distance away from the water. After roughly 300 metres the track passes an upright post on the right and crosses a small bridge over a minor side-stream (**GR 988 176**).

From here, count 220 paces as you walk along the track, to come to a point where it bends slightly to the left. **GR 985 177.**

The bend where you leave the track.

10. Here turn right to leave the track and go uphill, up the side of the ridge. As you get higher the top of the concrete trig point becomes visible in front. However, before heading directly for the trig, you should see something black sticking up from the ground just slightly to the left and head over towards it. When you get there you'll find that it is the remains of an old armoured vehicle. **GR 985 179.**

The remains of the old armoured vehicle.

During the Second World War, parts of Teesdale were used to train the crews of tanks and other armoured vehicles. The ranges at Battle Hill are a remnant of these training areas. The pieces left on the side of the hill are the remains of a military tracked vehicle. Sections of the tracks, bogie wheels and pieces of metal plate are laid in this boggy area. Unfortunately there are not enough remains to identify what type the vehicle actually was.

From the vehicle remains, resume your course back up to the trig point on Lamb Hill. The second and final trig point of the day. **GR 986 180.**

11. From the trig point head due north, towards the visible buildings of Booze Wood straight in front. As you descend and get closer to the farm, the car park in front of it will become clearer and your vehicle should come into view. Descend down to your car and then you can take your boots off and relax.

Following the side of the Tees after passing Woden Croft.
Walk4: A Teesdale Way Circular.

WALK 4: A TEESDALE WAY CIRCULAR

The Teesdale Way makes it's way from Dufton in Cumbria, across the Pennines and then follows the course of the River Tees downstream until it empties it's waters into the North Sea at Teesmouth. In many places the path makes it's way down both sides of the river at the same time and this walk utilises one of these sections to make a circular walk on either side of the river between Egglestone and Cotherstone and along the way discovers some hidden histories of the old dale..

DISTANCE: 5.4 miles / 8.7 km
ASCENT: 545 feet / 166 metres
TERRAIN: The bulk of this walk comprises field and meadow walking with a couple of short woodland paths. However, there is one section, as the path follows the Tees upstream, where the path is very rocky and in places skirts the water's edge. Here the path does undulate up and down the side of the bank and in places has been eroded by rain and floods. Because of the path's proximity to the river on this stretch then this walk should not be attempted in bad weather or at times of high water levels. There is no significant climbing on this route although there may be sections, when the path goes through woods and next to the river, where there may be short but steep climbs.
TIME: 4 to 4½ hours.
START: The village green in Romaldkirk. GR NY 994 220.
MAP: OL31. North Pennines. Teesdale and Weardale.
ACCESS: The route is all on public rights of way.
DOGS: As the route is all on public rights of way then dogs are allowed but as the majority of the route is through grazing meadows then you will encounter sheep and other livestock and so it is advisable to keep your dog on a lead. There are a number of tall stiles to lift your dog over and one section as the path runs next to the river will be a bit rocky underfoot for your pet. If you decide to visit the viewpoint of Percy Myres Rock then your dog will definitely need to be on a lead.

GRID REFERENCES

Romaldkirk village green	994 220
Path/road junction	996 232
Road/track junction	997 232
East Barnley Farm	008 222
Enclosure	010 212

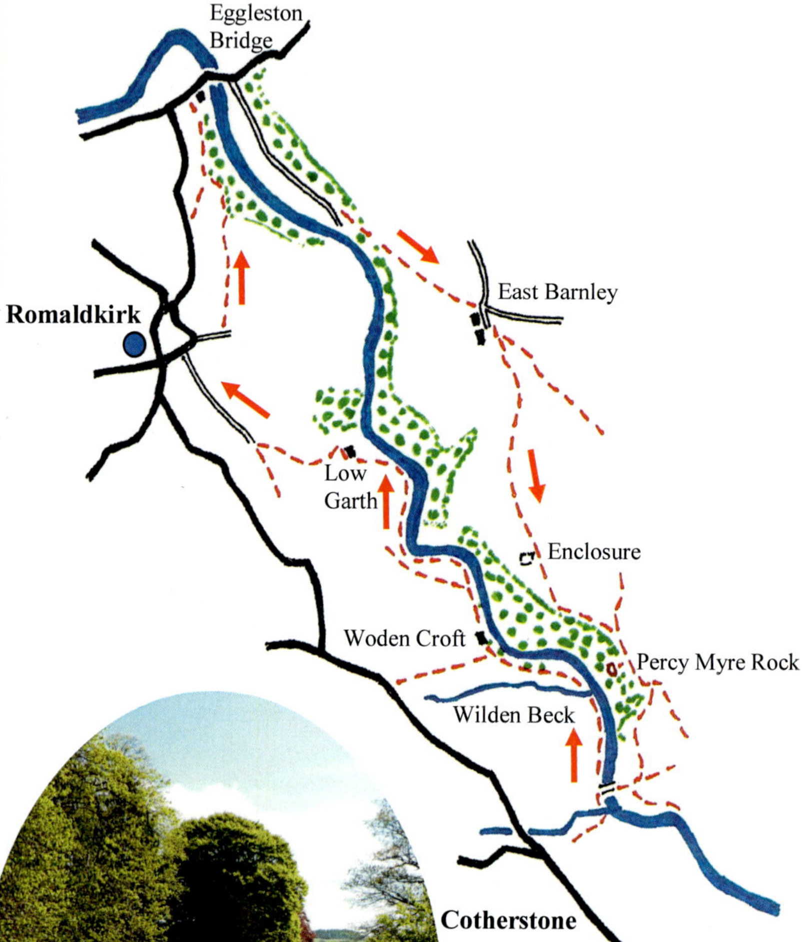

Following the road through the village to start the walk.

Percy Myres Rock	014 207
Footbridge	013 202
Woden Croft	008 207
Romaldkirk village green	994 220

FGS GRADING

Grading is T4 [D0, N1, T1, R1, H1]

Distance	**0**	Up to 6 miles
Navigation	**1**	Basic navigation skills needed
Terrain	**1**	50 – 75% on graded track or path, 25 – 50% off track
Remote-ness	**1**	Countryside in fairly close proximity to habitation – at least 80% of the route within 2 miles
Height	**1**	Over 100 ft per mile

THE WALK

1. Head in to the centre of Romaldkirk, going past both the Rose and Crown and the Kirk Inn. Then, when the road bends left, continue straight ahead down the dead-end lane. After a couple of hundred metres the lane branches and here continue straight ahead to come to a footpath signpost.

The entrance to the green lane across the little green.

At this signpost, turn left across the little green patch of grass and go down the green lane facing you. Follow the lane to come to a plank bridge over the nicely named Beer Beck. After crossing the beck you'll come to a stile in the left-hand wall. Cross and bear right across the field, heading for an electricity pole, and you'll find a stone stile just to the right of the pole.

Cross the stile and immediately turn right to follow the wall, keeping it on your right. When you get to the field corner, turn left to follow the fence line which eventually changes to a wall and here you need to turn to continue following the outside of the wall, again keeping it on your right. You'll then come to a stile, cross and continue following the wall which does change back to a fence as you follow it.

After a little while you'll come to a fence corner where the fence bends away to the right to head down towards the river. There is a very faded green marker attached to the fence here. At this point leave the fence to go straight ahead, making for the left of the small tree straight in front. Once over the low rise, make for the stone stile which stands to the left of the gate which, in turn, is to the left of the stone building. The stile leads on to the roadside. **GR 996 232.**

2. Turn right to follow the road down to the bridge over the river and about 40 metres after crossing the bridge, you'll come to a gated track on the right side of the road with a Teesdale Way signpost pointing up it. **GR 997 232.**

Eggleston Bridge is an old narrow sandstone bridge, the only one giving vehicle access across the Tees between Barnard Castle and Middleton-in-Teesdale. First built around 1450, the bridge was subsequently rebuilt during the 17th century, a rebuild that probably incorporated much of the earlier

Eggleston Bridge.

bridge. The bridge has two arches with, rather unusually, one being slightly pointed while the other is semi-circular. During the 15th century it is recorded that the rector of Romaldkirk, a John Newelyne, paid for a chapel to be built at the end of the bridge although, sadly, no remains of this can now be seen. Whether or not this chapel provided some divine intervention or not, but the bridge was one of the few in the area that survived the Great Flood of 1771.

3. Turn right to leave the road and go through the pedestrian gate next to the main gate. Follow the drive as it runs along the side of a small wood, after a little while it goes past a sports pavilion and then a couple of Boy's Brigade huts. Eventually the drive comes to a gate and there is a stile on the left.

Where the track ends at the gate, on the other side of the gate lies a small building which marks the end of the Kielder Tunnel. This tunnel carries water from the huge reservoir of Kielder Water, via the rivers Derwent, Tyne and Wear and into the Tees and is used to meet water shortfalls as and when necessary.

Turn left to cross the stile and then follow the path steeply up some steps and in to the woods. The path climbs up and then makes it's way through the woods. After a short while it descends to cross a stream, then climbs up the other side and goes through a small gate into a field.

The path now follows the right-hand wall along the bottom of the field. However, as you approach the end of the field the path then bears left to go a short way up the slope to a stone stile hidden in a kink of the wall that is facing you.

Cross the stile and then follow the path as it heads diagonally left up the slope of the field to the opposite corner where a fence and wall meet. As you get closer to the field corner, you'll start to see some buildings behind the trees and when you get to the corner itself, you'll find a gate and a waymarked stile. Cross the stile to follow the right-hand wall which will lead you to the front of the buildings of East Barnley where you'll join a track at a point next to an electricity post. **GR 008 222.**

4. Turn right to the track junction, which only lies a metre or two away, and then turn left for another metre or two to come to an electricity post with a waymarker on it. Here turn right to leave the track and follow the visible path across the field to a waymarked gate in the wall opposite.

Go through the gate and continue to follow the path as it heads across the field to a gate, stile and marker post on the opposite side, crossing a small stream just before you get to the wall. Cross and, following the direction of the marker post, head towards another stile and marker post that can be seen in the wall on the skyline. When you get there, cross and then bear slightly left to the waymarkers on the fence that lies a short distance away on top of the rise.

Once on top of the rise, turn right to follow the fence, keeping it on your left. After a short distance you'll pass a small fenced enclosure that lies just a few metres away below you. **GR 010 212.**

Despite the fence not being in perfect shape, the enclosure helps protect the remains of an Anglo-Saxon settlement dating back to the early Middle Ages. Underneath the grass the outline of the foundations of the building can be seen.

The enclosure surrounding the Anglo-Saxon settlement

5. Continue to follow the fence on the left to come to another gate, stile and marker post. Go through and you'll find that the fence is now on your right-hand side and borders the side of Shipley Wood. Continue to follow the side of the fence to yet another gate, stile and marker post.

Cross and follow the right-hand wall to come to a marker post that points straight ahead. Here you have a route choice, you can continue straight ahead or if you wish you can make a quick out and back diversion to see the viewpoint of Percy Myres Rock.

To visit the viewpoint, ignore the marker post and continue to follow the wall to come to a stile partially hidden behind a gorse bush. Cross the stile and the edge of the rock is a few metres away on the right. Take care as there are no fences or barriers between you and a long drop. **GR 014 207.**

Looking towards a distant Goldsborough and Shackleborough from Percy Myres Rock and, inset, the stile leading to the viewpoint.

6. Return back to the marker post and, following the direction shown by the post, go straight ahead over the small rise, keeping the stream and gully on the left. As you go down the other side of the rise you'll join a rough track and here bear left to cross the stream. Immediately after crossing the stream and before you come to the gate in front, turn right over a stone stile built into the wall to enter the wooded gully next to the stream. The path now goes between the wall and the gully and shortly comes to another stile that leads into a field.

Here bear right towards the gorse bushes and then follow the clear path through the bushes to come to a stile. Cross and continue on the path as it descends to enter a caravan park. Head straight across the park, which at this point is not very wide, to a visible gate on the other side. Go through the pedestrian gate next to the main gate and follow the track as it descends down to the riverside fields and when you get there, bear to the right and go towards a marker post and the metal Cotherstone footbridge over the River Tees. **GR 013 202.**

7. Cross the bridge and when on the other side, don't turn left to follow the main path but instead turn right to follow the path by the river. The path doesn't stick by the river for long and soon climbs up to a stile leading into a field.

Cross and follow the path across the field keeping a short distance away from the fence on the right. The path leads to another stile that brings you back into the trees bordering the river. After you have crossed the stile, the path follows

The Cotherstone footbridge was built in 1932 and while it's lattice girder framework is functional, it can not necessarily be considered a 'pretty' bridge. This is the third bridge on the site, the original being a timber construction that was replaced after it was damaged during floods in 1881 but it was the second bridge that was both the most elegant and the most notorious. Built to replace the damaged timber bridge, the second Cotherstone footbridge was a suspension bridge that, by the use of cables, spanned the rocky gorge from one side of the river to the other. As with most suspension bridges, it was slim and elegant, lacking the bulk of a bridge built around a framework of girders like the current one. It stood for 48 years until the accident happened.

Good Friday, 1929 and a football match was being played between the two teams from the local villages of Cotherstone and Mickleton. The pitch upon which the game was being played on was on the northern side of the river, opposite Cotherstone, and with it being a Good Friday holiday and there being, obviously, local rivalry between the two villages, the match was very well attended. At the end of the game the leaving crowd crossed the bridge on their way back to Cotherstone. With forty people on the bridge, one of the supporting cables snapped and plunged the structure into the rocky waters below. Twenty of the people crossing were flung into the water but desperate help from both sides of the river prevented anybody drowning. However one young woman was seriously injured during the collapse and subsequently died of her injuries.

As you cross the bridge try to imagine what it would feel like to be flung down into the river below as the bridge collapses beneath you. Small wonder why they built a sturdier replacement a couple of years later.

the fence which is now on your left, and descends to cross the Wilden Beck via some concrete stepping stones. They look a bit dodgy but they are actually safer than they look.

Once on the other side, cross a stile into a field and here leave the fence on the right to head up and over the rise in front that has a covering of trees and is to the right of the beck. As you go over the rise, a stone wall and building will appear in front of you, head to the right side of the wall where you will find a waymarker and a short lane that leads to a gate. Go through the gate and continue straight ahead to another gate at the left of the buildings where there is a marker post. **GR 008 207.**

8. Don't go through the gate but instead turn right through the gate on that side and follow the fence, keeping it on your left, to go past the buildings of Woden Croft and head towards a barn. A waymarker directs you to the right of the barn and to a gate and stile. Cross and follow the right-hand fence to the end of the field where you will come to another gate and stile.

Ignore the marker on the gate that points to the left and continue to follow the wall, which is now on your right, a short distance to yet another gate and stile, this one entering the woods that border the river. The path now descends

As you make your way over the rocks you may notice hollows and holes in the rocks themselves. Known locally as the fairy cupboards and once thought to be the homes of the 'little folk', in reality the small caves were created by the scouring action of the river.

through the woods to the side of the river where it now shadows the water up-stream. As it follows the side of the river, sections of the path get a bit rocky and in one or two places you have to pick your way through the riverside boulders.

Eventually the path climbs away from the river and comes to a gate and stile leading into a field. Cross the stile and then follow the right-hand wall for about 100 metres, before the path then bears left towards the buildings of Low Garth. Go to the left of the ruined buildings, keeping them on your right, to come to a gate and stile.

Go over the stile onto a track and follow it as it goes past the buildings and then bears left to go up the hillside. Don't follow the track all the way up to the gate but instead, at the top of the bend, leave the right-side of the track to go up to a small, waymarked pedestrian gate partially hidden in the hedge, just to the left of the tree.

Go through the gate and then go straight ahead to another waymarked gate in the hedge on the opposite side of the field, the gate lying to the right of a tree. Once through this gate, go straight ahead over the rise and then make for the clump of trees where you will find a wooden gate leading into a walled lane.

Heading towards the clump of trees and, inset, heading down the lane back to Romaldkirk.

This lane is then followed back to Romaldkirk.

Looking back down Red Grooves Hush.
Walk 5: Red Grooves Hush and Coldberry Gutter.

COLDBERRY GUTTER

Coldberry Gutter is a highly visible scar in the watershed between the neighbouring valleys of the Hudeshope and Bow Lee becks. It is the largest and most spectacular hush in the North Pennines and is a dominant landscape feature that is visible from many miles away. The hush itself runs for 1.7 km as it cuts it's way through Hardberry Hill and in places is up to 50 metres wide with a depth into the hillside of 30 metres. However, at either end of the hush lie extensive mining grounds, the Red Grooves mines to the west and the Coldberry mines to the east.

Deep within the hush.

The early history of these lead workings is uncertain but more than two million tons of ore and rock had been removed from the hush in the years leading up to the mid-1700's. An extensive network of levels and shafts then worked the veins under the hills during the 19th century. With the collapse of the lead market in the early 1900's the mines declined although one vein at the Coldberry end of the hush was worked from the late 1930's, finally closing in 1953.

As you descend down the east end of the hush, you pass the remains of the Coldberry Mine driven into the hillside by the London Lead Company in the mid-1800's. As part of this complex there is a two-storey lodging shop, a stable and blacksmith's shop, a level entrance and a powder store used for storing explosives. All of these are Grade II listed buildings and have been restored by the North Pennines Heritage Trust.

The hush is part of a scheduled ancient monument that includes the remains and workings of the Coldberry Mine at the eastern end and also the remains and workings of the Red Grooves Mines at the western end of the hush plus the

Coldbery Shop and, inset, the entrance to the Coldberry Level.

extensive water management system of leats, dams and reservoirs on either side of the hush that gathered the water that was the power source of the mining machinery.

WALK 5: RED GROOVES HUSH AND COLDBERRY GUTTER

Just north of Middleton-in-Teesdale lies the small side-valley of the Hudeshope Beck. During the 18th and 19th centuries this little dead-end valley was a hive of industrial activity as men from Middleton and the surrounding area toiled both above and below ground wresting lead ore from the rocks of this valley.

DISTANCE: 6.9 mile / 11.1 km.
ASCENT: 968 feet / 295 metres.
TERRAIN: The first section of this walk is a rather lengthy road walk of nearly three miles after which a moorland track is followed to get to the bottom of Red Grooves Hush. From there, walking up the hush and down Coldberry Gutter is the equivalent of walking over the open moor and well within the capability of the average hill walker. After Coldberry Shop, field paths and a quiet country road are followed back to Middleton. The climbing in this walk is more long

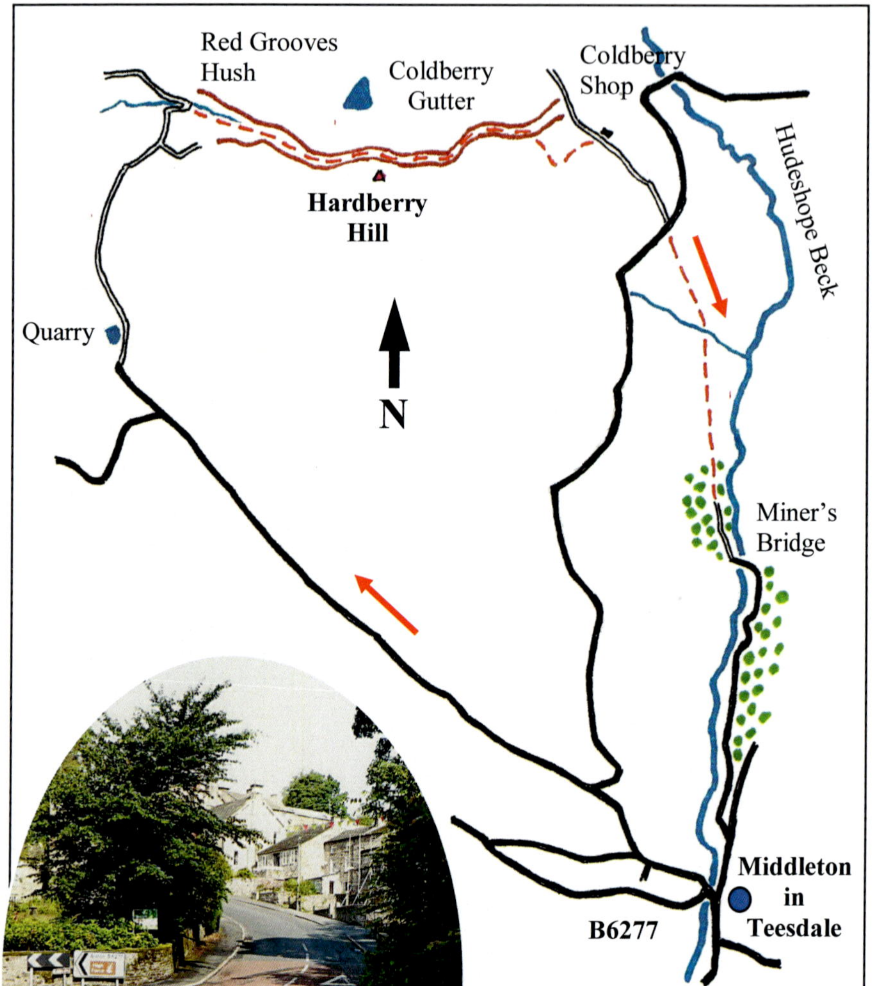

Start of walk - Market place, Middleton-in-Teesdale.

Inset. At the start of the walk, heading up the side road after crossing the bridge over the Hudeshope Beck,

and steady rather than short and steep.
TIME: 4½ hours
START: Middleton-in-Teesdale market place. GR NY 947 254.
MAP: OL31. North Pennines. Teesdale and Weardale.
ACCESS: Most of the route is on public rights of way, however, the middle, linking section that goes over Red Grooves Hush and Coldberry Gutter is on access land.
DOGS: Not allowed on the access land.

GRID REFERENCES

Middleton market place	947 254
Road corner	922 278
Bridge	923 291
Kissing gate	931 290
Level	940 290
Coldberry Shop	942 290
Roadside	944 286
Level	947 275
Bridge	948 271
Middleton market place	947 254

FGS GRADING
Grading is F6 [D1, N1, T1, R1, H2]

Distance	**1**	6 – 12 miles
Navigation	**1**	Basic navigation skills needed
Terrain	**1**	50 – 75% on graded track or path, 25 – 50% off track
Remote-ness	**1**	Countryside in fairly close proximity to habitation – at least 80% of the route within 2 miles
Height	**2**	Over 125 ft per mile

THE WALK

1. From the market place follow the main B6277 road towards Alston, heading up the dale. Ignore the side road going off to Stanhope on the right, and continue to cross the bridge over the Hudeshope Beck. Once over the bridge the road turns sharply left and here leave it to go up the side road immediately in front that climbs quite steeply up the bank.

Follow the road up the hill, passing as you go the Raby Estate Yard and then a little later the large and grand Middleton House. As you leave the houses of the village behind, you'll pass two side junctions on the left side of the road and a short while later one on the right side signposted to Aukside and Coldberry.

Continue to follow the road ahead and not long after passing the junction on the right, the climb levels off. Although the prospect of walking a couple of miles along a road isn't normally appealing, this walk along a very quiet lane running half way up one side of the dale is actually the reverse with some outstanding views up the dale..

Eventually, after about an hours walking since leaving Middleton, you'll come to a corner where the main road turns sharply left and a dead-end tarmac lane continues straight ahead. **GR 922 278.**

The old spoil heaps above the road.

At this point if you look over the wall on the right, you can see the tell-tale shapes of old spoil heaps further up the side of the hill. Along most of the hillside above the road there has been the scars of mining activity but most have been out of sight above the edge of the hill. It's not long now before you start to get a bit closer to the remains of the old lead mining.

2. Continue straight ahead down the dead-end lane and when you get to the end, bear right following the track indicated by the bridleway signpost to come, after a short distance, to a gate. Pass through the gate and the track now goes round an old flooded quarry on the left while over on the right an old lime kiln lies within a small fenced enclosure. Continue on the track to come to another gate and after passing through this, the track continues before coming to a third beyond which lies a couple of very large spoil heaps.

Go through the gate and ignore the faint track that goes off on the right, to continue straight ahead following the main track as it descends slightly and turns to the right to pass between the two spoil heaps. As you go between the heaps, the valley floor of a small stream becomes visible.

This is the country of the Red Grooves Hushes, once a hive of activity as the men of the dale worked the lead ore from the grip of the hillside.

Continue on the track as it bends round to come to a bridge over the small stream. **GR 923 291.**

Passing the spoil heaps and, inset, approaching the bridge.

3. Don't cross the bridge but instead bear right to follow the right bank of the stream up into the hush itself.

As you follow the stream you'll notice that in places it has been covered over and it flows through long culverts. In a narrow valley like this, it was probably done to make flat working areas, something that would be in short supply. When you reach the end of the last culvert, to the right of the path, hidden in a patch of vegetation, lies the partially covered-in remains of a level entrance. Although structurally similar to the mouths of the culverts, this is "dry" with no stream running out of it and heads directly into the side of the hill.

The route now follows the floor of the main hush as it climbs up to go over

Hardberry Hill. Although in the early stages there are a couple of side hushes going off either side, it is fairly easy to tell which is the main hush as it makes it's way up the hill. The walking itself is also not too bad, easier than what you would first think but bear in mind that this was originally a working site and men would have had to make their way up here each and every day. There are one or two spots where the slope has been eroded away and is a little bit steep but it is nothing that the average walker couldn't cope with. If at any point you do feel a little bit uncertain, it is quite easy to retrace your steps a little bit and climb up the right bank and then follow the hush from above it.

Heading up the hush.

After a while the narrowness of the hush is somewhat relieved as it opens out into a wider space and here a track comes in from the right. You are now nearing the top of the hill, so continue following the hush straight ahead through the deep gash cut into the hill.

As you walk, it is worthwhile to keep turning round for a look. The views back down the hush into the Tees valley are quite something.

When you reach the crest of the hush, where the climbing from Teesdale stops and the descent into Hudeshope starts, you'll come to a fence line and a kissing gate. **GR 931 290.**

4. Go through the kissing gate and continue to follow the hush as it now makes it's way downhill. After a little while, a small stream starts to flow down the middle of the hush. Stay on the right side of the stream and as close to it as you can. Resist the urge to go up the side of the bank in order to keep your feet dry, the bank gets a bit steeper a bit further on and you'll only have to retrace your steps back down to the side of the stream.

Stay by the stream side despite the boggy bits and eventually the narrowness of the hush will begin to open out and in front of you will appear two spoil heaps. By all means walk out along the top of the heaps, they do present a grand view of the valley of the Hudeshope Beck and, a short distance away to the right, the building of Coldberry Shop, which is your next target to aim for. You will also see to the right, running round the front of the hill, a faint path.

The front of the spoil heaps are too steep to go down so retrace your steps along them and go down the right side so that the heaps are now in-between you and the stream. Keeping the heap on your left, continue downhill and you'll come to the start of the path that curves round the front of the hill that you saw from the top of the heap. The start of the path is marked by a number of metal posts standing proud above ground level.

Heading down the side of the spoil heaps and, inset, the path beside the leat.

The metal posts are in fact short sections of rail tracks that were used to move tubs of lead ore within the mines. The posts actually sit within what was called a leat, a man-made channel for funnelling water. Water was an essential element in the processing of lead ore, from using water power to move the crushing wheels to using it to separate the heavier lead from the lighter rock. Great expense and trouble was taken to ensure that there was an adequate, reliable water supply for the mines and in many cases this entailed leats crossing miles of open moor. In some cases, as with this one, the leat would have a cover of stone slabs to try and prevent the water freezing during winter.

The path follows the side of the leat as it curves round the front of the hill. Stay on the path until you have come to a deep hush and here leave the path and leat to follow the left side of the hush down to the clearly seen building of Coldberry Shop.

The descent is easy walking and as you get towards the bottom of the hush a faint path develops which then bears right at the bottom to head over to the Shop. As you get to the bottom of the hush you'll notice that there are stretches of stonework lining it's sides. Take a look, the stonework forms part of the entrance portal of Richardson's Level. **GR 940 290.**

Following the hush down to Coldberry Shop and, inset, the entrance of Richardson's Level.

The path now heads directly for the Shop which is only a couple of hundred metres away, crossing as it does some soft and boggy ground, to come to a gate leading onto the track next to the Shop. **GR 942 290.**

5. Turn right onto the track and follow it past the Coldberry Level entrance until you come to a roadside. **GR 944 286.**

6. At the roadside, turn right to cross the cattle grid and make for the marker post a few metres away on the left side of the road. Cross the stile and, following the direction indicated by the marker post, head diagonally over the field on a well-walked path to a wall stile.

This stile has a "bull" sign on it but it is a well-walked path and there are no real problems. Once across the stile follow the path across the field, the field itself is quite wide and half-way across you have to descend a deep gully to cross the

Clubgill Sike. When you are over, continue across the field and on the other side you'll cross a narrow stream and come to a wall stile with a bright yellow waymarker next to it.

Go over the stile and you'll now cross two narrow fields to come into a third. In this third field, the path heads towards the trees on the opposite side and just as you approach them, descends over the edge of a small valley to come to a ladder stile leading in to the wood.

Follow the path down through the trees. In places the path is stepped but whoever built the steps must be expecting people with long legs. After a short distance the path comes down to the side of a stream and a fence. At this point, on the other side of the fence lies the entrance of Aukside Level. **GR 947 275.** A better view can be obtained by following the fence and path down to a step stile and once on the other side following the fence back up to the entrance.

The entrance to the wet level and below, the dry level.

From the step stile, the path comes to a plank bridge going over the stream. However, before you cross it, bear left to go over the flow of water coming out of the level entrance and go a few metres down the path to where a tree grows out of the side of it. Here, next to the tree and hidden so that the path runs over the top of it, lies the "dry" entrance to the level that you have just visited round the corner.

Return back to the plank bridge and cross it. The path heads down through the trees and as it slightly descends becomes more of a track. After a short while the track is blocked by a gate, go round it and on to a bridge. **GR 948 271.**

Many mines were built with two entrances, one termed "wet" and one "dry". A constant problem in mining was water and the draining out of the workings so that they wouldn't be flooded. One solution was to drive the horizontal shaft in to the hillside at a slight upwards angle so that the water would naturally flow out. The level serving as both an entrance and a drain. The problem with this is that anybody walking into the mine would have to do so through the water. So many mines also had a "dry" entrance with no stream of water gushing out. Despite appearances this was not done for the benefit of the miners but rather for the ponies that worked in the mines hauling the tubs of ore. Spending time constantly in water made them susceptible to foot ailments especially hoof-rot.

7. Cross the bridge onto a tarmac road and follow this as it makes it's way down the left bank of the Hudeshope Beck. Despite another "road walk" the route down this valley is very picturesque with the rugged bed of the beck cutting it's way through the rock on the right and both road and beck being surrounded by trees.

Not too long after you've started to follow the road, it crosses a bridge over a side-stream and here passes a small ruined building on the left. Again another reminder of the lead mining days, this used to be a powder house where explosives for use in the mines were kept. Far enough away so that no damage could be caused by "accidents" but in a position where the miners could pick up the explosives on their way up to the mines.

The old explosives store.

Continue along the road and eventually it starts to climb, leaving the beck below it and comes to a junction with another road on the outskirts of Middleton. Here turn right to follow this road back down in to the centre of the village.

The trig point on Citron Seat.
Walk 6: Citron Seat and Seven Hills.

WALK 6: CITRON SEAT AND SEVEN HILLS

Carved by the Stainmore Glacier during the last Ice Age, the Stainmore Gap is a relatively low-level pass between the higher hills of the Pennines lying to the north and south. For thousands of years man has used this pass to travel from one side of this mountain range to the other. Situated on the eastern side of this pass, the small village of Bowes has long been the guardian of the eastern entrance. The remains of two forts, Roman and Norman, provide testimony to it's strategic importance.

This walk explores the low hills to the south of the village, an area that is not that often visited by the walker. Here the hills may be low but they provide extensive views through the Gap itself and to the higher hills both north and south. The walk also takes the opportunity to visit the long-forgotten lead mine of the Eller Beck.

DISTANCE: 7.4 mile / 11.8 km
ASCENT: 1,161 feet / 354 metres
TERRAIN: The majority of this walk is over moorland paths some of which are quite boggy irrespective of which time of year you walk this route and some which have the habit of appearing and disappearing amongst the heather and reeds. At times you may wonder if you are actually following a path at all. There are no particularly steep climbs on this walk, they tend to be more long and steady.
TIME: 4½ hours
START: Bowes and Gilmonby Village Hall car park. GR NY 996 135.
MAP: OL31 North Pennines. Teesdale and Weardale.
ACCESS: The route is a mixture of public rights of way and open access land. Although most of the route over the moor is on rights of way, the descent down to Eller Beck Mine and the descent down off the moor after Citron Seat are over open access land.
DOGS: Not allowed on the access land.

GRID REFERENCES

Car park	996 135
Road junction	995 127
Road/bridleway junction	992 124
Wall corner	999 110
Gate	994 107
Eller Beck Mine	992 103
Citron Seat	978 102
Gate	973 102
Path/road junction	967 113
Gate	967 122

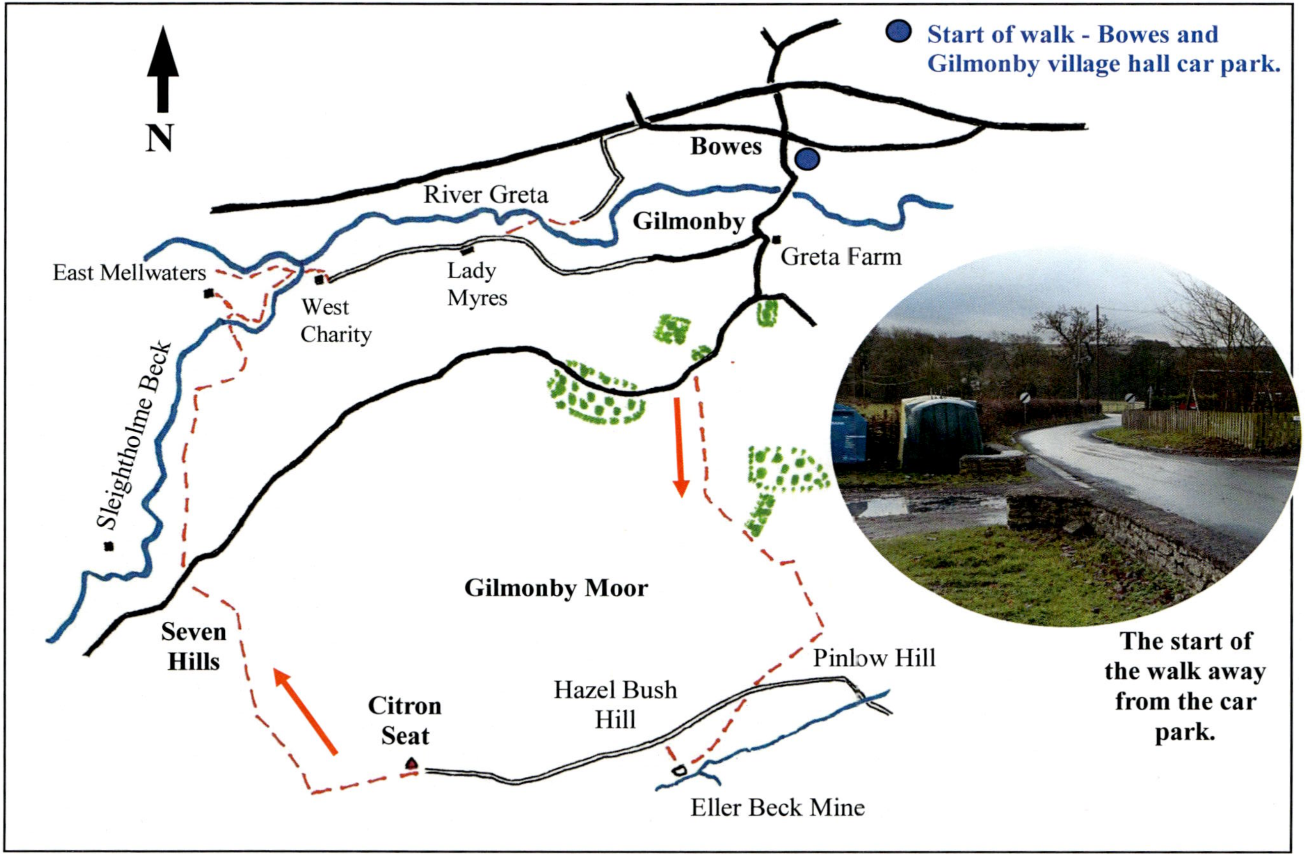

The start of the walk away from the car park.

Cardwell Bridge	972 128
Car park	996 135

FGS GRADING

Grading is F8 [D1, N1, T2, R2, H2]

Distance	**1**	6 – 12 miles
Navigation	**1**	Basic navigation skills needed
Terrain	**2**	25 -50% on graded track or path, 50 – 75% off track
Remoteness	**2**	Countryside not in close proximity to habitation – less than 20% of the route within 2 miles
Height	**2**	Over 125 ft per mile

THE WALK

1. From the car park turn left to follow the road downhill towards Gilmonby. At the bottom of the bank cross the bridge over the River Greta and continue following the road up the bank on the other side to enter the small hamlet of Gilmonby. Here ignore the road going off on the right, signposted Home Farm and West Gates, to go straight ahead passing Greta Farm on the left. The road starts to climb now as it heads up towards a small wood, coming to a junction just in front of it. **GR 995 128.**

Gilmonby Bridge, an early 18th century road bridge over the River Greta.

2. Turn right to follow the signpost to Sleightholme with the road still climbing as it bends to the right. After a while the road approaches another small wood on the right while on the left side stands an old corrugated metal barn. Just after passing the barn, you'll come to a bridleway signpost on the left side of the road pointing through a gate. **GR 992 124.**

The bridleway sign and gateway.

3. Here leave the road to turn left through the gate and then go straight ahead to follow the left hand wall and come to another gate at the end of the field, this one having the open access brown walking man on it. Go through and, again, continue straight ahead this time following the fence on the left to come to a third gate, this one waymarked.

Pass through the gate and turn to follow the left-hand wall. Shortly you'll cross a small stream, How Low Gill, that runs through the wall but stay away from the deep shake hole that is fenced off over to the right. Continue to follow the wall to just past the woods that butt onto the other side of it. Here the map shows the bridleway bearing right over the moor but there is no sign of this on the ground. As the open moor is quite difficult terrain to cross, you're actually better off continuing to follow the wall on the left. There is a rough path to follow through the long grass and reeds although it is rather boggy and quite often disappears. Eventually you'll come to a wall corner. **GR 999 110.**

As you follow the wall, the views on the left, down and across the Tees Valley are very far-reaching.

4. Once in the wall corner, turn right to follow the wall, keeping the wall on your left, as it makes it's way up Pinlow Hill. The walking now is a lot easier as a wide, dry, visible path shadows the side of the wall. After a steady climb, you'll come to a gate in the wall. **GR 994 107.**

5. Go through the gate and straight across the heather on the other side to join the side of a track that lies just a few metres away from the gate.

Here you have a route option, if you wish to go directly to Citron Seat then turn right to follow the track as it climbs the hill. However, if you wish to visit the Eller Beck Mine first, then go straight across the track and start to descend into the valley below. As you descend, bear to the right to make your way down the bank while heading upstream.

Heading down to the side of the Eller Beck and, inset, the stream gushing out of the hole in the rock face.

Once you have reached the side of the bank, turn right to follow it upstream to come to a point where the water divides. The main stream turns left and heads towards the sheer wall of a small cliff face. It is actually worth following to see the water gushing out of a small hole cut into the rock.

Back at the stream junction, the minor stream heads up the main hush, while the distinctive gash of a second hush lies cut into the rock face on the right. Head towards this right-hand hush to find the main entrance to the mine.

Once finished at the site of the mine, head back up the side of the hill to the track that you crossed after you came through the gate and once on it, turn left to follow it as it makes it's way up over Hazel Bush Hill towards the distant trig point of Citron Seat. Just before you get to the trig, the track ends in a turning

ELLERBECK LEAD MINE

Not a lot is known about the Ellerbeck mine. Unlike the upper reaches of the dale, the lower parts of Teesdale were not significantly rich in mineral deposits despite the fact that this part of the dale lies 'just the other side of the hill' to the extremely rich Arkengarthdale ore field. However, a number of small mines were driven into the side of the hill in an attempt to exploit those riches that did exist.

The entrance to the main level in front of the hush.

The mine at Ellerbeck was probably started in the early 1800's, most likely around 1830, and was in operation for only around seventy years until 1901. Unlike other mines in Arkengarthdale and Teesdale, Ellerbeck was only a small operation and may not have been continuously operated during this period.

The workings themselves comprise a 300 metre long hush which was effectively open cast working for ore where the lead vein was dug out from the surface. There are also three small levels or adits which were used to access the vein at lower levels than could be reached by hushing. On the side of the hill above the mine, lie six old shafts which were also used to access the lower levels of the vein.

circle but it is just a short walk on a distinctive path up to Citron Seat itself. **GR 978 102.**

Before you leave the summit of Citron, have a good look at the top. This is more or less perfectly round, very reminiscent of a round spot placed on top of the moor. Probably natural, possibly a glacial drumlin formed from deposits left behind from when the Stainmore Glacier cut through these hills during the last Ice Age, but if you do notice it, then it does get the mind working.

6. From the Seat continue to follow the wall on the right, westwards. Although there is a path of sorts next to the wall, the going is a great deal rougher than the track that you have just left. After a little while, and just before you come to a wall corner, you'll come to both a kissing gate and a small gate in the wall on the right. **GR 973 102.**

7. Turn right to go through the kissing gate and you'll find another wall, again on the right-hand side. A rough path now follows the side of the wall through the long grass. The ground here is the gathering point for a number of small streams that flow down to join the Sleightholme Beck and so is fairly boggy plus the path does keep disappearing and reappearing as you make your way through the moor grass.

The path and the wall head towards the low mounds of Seven Hills and here, as the path runs between the hills on the left and the wall on the right, you pick up the track of a quad bike which makes the going that little bit easier. The quad track now follows the wall down off the moor to come to the side of a road. **GR 967 113.**

Heading towards the low mounds of Seven Hills.

Seven Hills is a grouping of what are a number of low hills, again very probably drumlins formed by glacial deposits. The hills themselves are not much more than bumps on the ground and the number that you can actually count depends very much on where you are standing and what you think constitutes a hill.

8. On the right lies a cattle grid and a bridleway signpost, cross the cattle grid and leave the road at the signpost to follow a visible path through the long grass. The path heads northwards above the edge of the valley of the Sleightholme Beck as the beck heads down to the wooded gorge known as The Trough.

The path comes to a wall and gate and here go through to follow the path straight ahead. As you cross the field, you'll approach a wall and here, just before you reach the wall, the path bends left to descend down to a waymarked gate. **GR 967 122.**

9. Pass through the gate and continue straight ahead along the side of the hill and after a few hundred metres bear left to descend down to the footbridge over the beck that you can see below you. Cross the bridge and turn right and, ignoring the waymarked gate up the bank, turn right again down the gravel track to follow the side of the beck. The path takes you through the fields bordering the stream to come to the Cardwell Bridge that crosses it. **GR 972 127.**

The Meeting of the Waters and, inset, the Cardwell Bridge.

After you have crossed the bridge look to your left to see the Meeting of the Waters, where the

Sleightholme Beck joins the River Greta. This joining of the two water courses also gives the name 'Mellwaters'.

10. Cross the bridge and then head to the left of West Charity Farm, which lies in front, to come to a signposted gate. Here turn right, following the Pennine Way, to follow the track straight ahead and through the yard to another signpost. The track now turns left to head through the fields towards Lady Mires Farm passing through two gateways as it goes.

As you walk along this stretch, keep your eyes open for views of Bowes Castle rising between the trees in front of you.

Pass through the gate in front of the farm and continue along the track with the farm on your right. A couple of hundred metres after the farm, a Pennine Way signpost directs you left off the track and through a gate towards a visible footbridge that takes you across the River Greta.

When you are over the bridge, turn right to follow the river bank for a few metres before leaving it to head for the bottom of a lane that heads up the bank on the left. Go up the lane, passing Swinholme Farm, and go through the gate after the farm.

The track now turns left and on this stretch, ignore the Pennine Way signpost on the right to stay on the track. The track then turns right to come to an access road. Here turn right to head towards Bowes, going round a gate on the way, and when you come to the road junction, continue straight ahead to come into the top end of the village. Stay on the road through the village to come to the roundabout with the village hall car park on the right.

High Force from the south bank viewpoint and, inset, Bleabeck Force.
Walk 7: Waterfalls and Ancient Settlements.

WALK 7: WATERFALLS AND ANCIENT SETTLEMENTS

Teesdale is noted for it's waterfalls with the surging waters of the Tees boiling over rocky outcrops as it makes it's way downstream. Indeed, this is where the name Tees comes from, from the ancient Celtic and relates to the Welsh 'Tes' with the meaning 'boiling, surging river'. Here many of these torrents bear the name 'force', a remnant from the days when the Vikings settled this region, 'fors' being Old Norse for waterfall. As you can tell from the history of the names within the dale, this valley has a long past much of which goes unnoticed unless you know what to look for. This walk mixes both waterfalls and the remains of ancient settlements that span the long history of man's occupation of this dale.

DISTANCE: 7.8 miles / 12.5 km.
ASCENT: 778 feet / 237 metres.
TERRAIN: Initially the route follows a field track to Dirt Pit before going over a couple of field paths to the roadside and then following the roadside pavement for a short distance. Paths over rough pasture are then followed to a bridge crossing of the River Tees and then the Pennine Way is followed alongside the river back to the Wynch Bridge and a crossing of the river back to Bowlees. The Pennine Way is a mixture of open moorland, rough pasture and riverside paths but despite being well-walked can be a bit soft and boggy in places. There is one short but steep climb up through the crags after passing Cronkley Farm but all the other climbs are more gradual and not that significant.
TIME: 4 to 4½ hours.
START: Bowlees Car Park. GR NY 907 283.
MAP: This route is on OL31 North Pennines although it is split over both sides of the map.
ACCESS: The route is all on public rights of way.
DOGS: As the route is all on rights of way then dogs are allowed but keep them under close control, preferably on a leash. Livestock, especially sheep, will be encountered throughout the walk plus you will also go through or pass farmyards where other dogs will probably be encountered. There are a number of stiles on the walk that may require you to lift your dog over.

Grid References

Bowlees car park	907 283
Track/road junction	891 289
High Force Hotel	885 286
Road junction	881 289

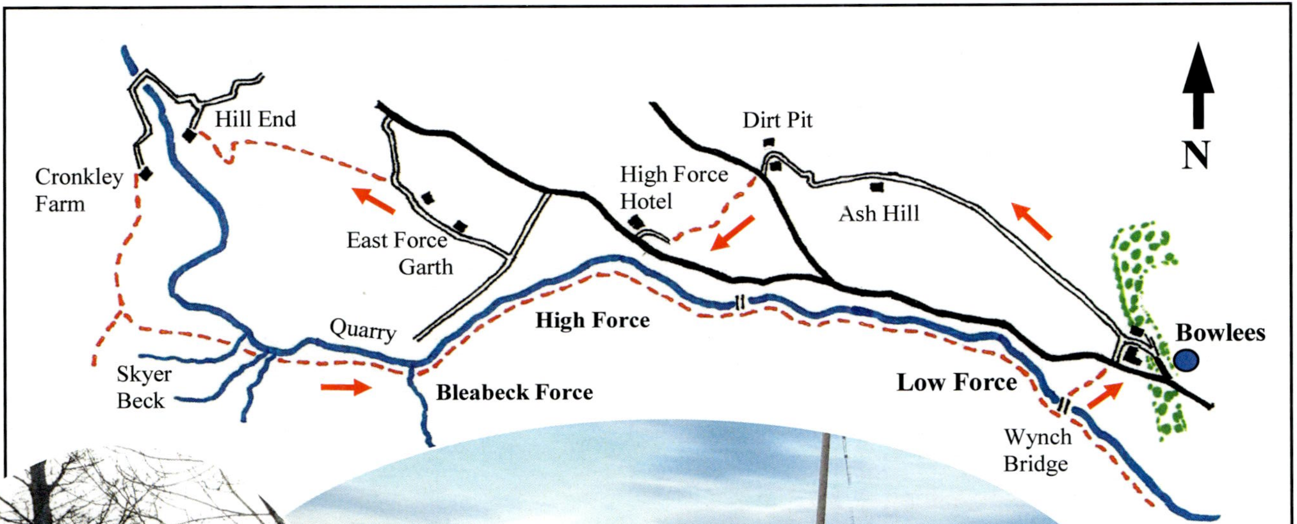

The start of the track heading to Dirt Pit.

Gateway	874 289
Bridge	862 294
Slag heap	867 281
Prehistoric settlement	871 280
Holwick Head Bridge	889 283
Wynch Bridge	904 279
Bowlees car park	907 283

FGS Grading

Grading is F6 [D1, N1, T2, R1, H1]

Distance	**1**	6 – 12 miles
Navigation	**1**	Basic navigation skills needed
Terrain	**2**	25 -50% on graded track or path, 50 – 75% off / single track
Remoteness	**1**	Countryside in fairly close proximity to habitation – at least 80% of the route within 2 miles
Height	**1**	Over 100 ft per mile

THE WALK

1. From the car park cross the bridge over the Bowlees Beck and go up the steps to follow the path to the Visitor Centre. Somehow ignore the delights of the café, they'll wait until you get back, and go down the side of the building to the front of the centre. Here turn right to a gated track with a signpost proclaiming the way to the High Force Hotel and Dirt Pit.

This track leading to Dirt Pit was once the main valley road leading from Middleton to Forest-in-Teesdale. It was replaced by the current road in 1820.

Go through the gate and, ignoring the side track on the right, follow the track as it goes straight ahead through a number of small fields and slowly climbs towards a small barn on the skyline. As you go through the gate next to the barn, ignore the footpath direction post on the right to continue following the track next to the left-hand wall. After a little while you'll pass the entrance to West Common Farm on the left and the track then comes to Ash Hill where, again, you ignore the bridleway marker post on the right to continue on the track.

The track now starts to descend down to the white buildings of Dirt Pit passing as it does a footpath marker and a stile on the left.

Approaching Dirt Pit.

Although not exactly modern, the farm and buildings of Dirt Pit are built on an even earlier settlement. Between 1161 and 1167 Bernard de Balliol granted parcels of land in Teesdale to the monks of Rievaulx Abbey which is situated near Helmsley on the edge of the North York Moors. At the time one method of ensuring salvation was to make gifts to religious orders to prove your piety and Rievaulx was one of the richest and most influential abbeys in the north of England. These grants included the right to graze horses and establish a stud near to Middleton and to also establish a cattle ranch at the nearby Ettersgill. Being an order of monks there was a need to provide religious guidance to the lay-brothers and foresters who worked these lands, and so a chapel was established and maintained at Dirt Pit.

The name Dirt Pit itself is a corruption of the words 'deer path' which reflects it's location amongst what was the Forest of Teesdale. On a map dating back to 1576, it was named as Durtpit Chapel.

Go through the gate in front of Dirt Pit and follow the track as it goes between the buildings and then bears left and crosses Ettersgill Beck, with a small waterfall on the right-hand side of the bridge. You'll now approach a V-junction and here go straight on to meet the side of a road. **GR 891 289.**

2. Turn right to the footpath marker post and stile which is just a couple of metres away. Cross into the field and then head towards the narrow bridge over a small stream that lies just in front. When you're across, continue on the path which goes roughly straight ahead towards a visible marker post and then continue over the rise to a waymarked gate in the right-hand wall.

Go through the gate and then head to the right of the small barn towards a visible footpath sign on the other side of the field. When you have crossed the field, go through the metal gate and then cross the stile on the left. You'll now find yourself above the High Force car park, so follow the left side of the fence down, bear right through the gateway and cross the car park to come to the roadside in front of the High Force Hotel. **GR 885 286.**

3. Taking care, cross the road and turn right to follow the footpath alongside the road, going past the entrance to the waterfall, for around 450 metres until you come to a side road on the left that goes to Force Garth Quarry, with a footpath signpost pointing up it. **GR 881 289.**

4. Turn left down the side road and follow it under the height restriction barrier and up the rise on the other side and as you come to the top of the rise you'll come to a track on the right that heads up to East Force Garth Farm which can be seen a short distance away on the skyline. Despite the fact that there are no waymarkers or signposts to show that you are on the right route, turn right here to follow the track up to the farm.

As you head up towards the farm, the track goes between two fields, both of which have large numbers of loose stones on the surface of the ground. These stones are the remains of a Romano-British settlement, a native British Celtic

The line of a wall on the right-side of the track.

settlement during the period of Roman occupation. Look close and within the stones you can see the outline of rubble banked walls enclosing small, irregular shaped fields and within, a complex of circular, oval and rectangular buildings. The site was excavated between 1972 and 1974 with a number of artefacts being recovered and is now a scheduled ancient monument.

Go through the gate in front of the farm and continue to follow the track as it passes to the left of the buildings and then, once behind, it bears right and continues to West Force Garth Farm. Ignore the track on the right that goes down to the farm and continue straight ahead, above the farm, to come to a gateway. **GR 874 289.**

5. Go through the gate and here leave the track to turn left and follow the wall as it goes between the two low crags of High and Low Knott. As you go between the two outcrops, you'll crest the ridge and find in front of you a panorama of the upper reaches of Teesdale. Here you should pick up a rough quad track which runs a little distance away from the wall and follow this to come to a metal gate.

Go through and the track now bears left to follow the wall on that side. Ignore the gate that can be seen on the opposite side of the narrow field and stay on the track for another couple of hundred metres. Then, as the track starts to descend to a gate in the left-hand wall, leave the track to cross the field to a visible stile in the wall on the right-side of the field.

Cross the stile and follow the left-hand wall to Hill End Farm, which lies just a short distance in front, and when you get there join a track at the side of the buildings. Turn right to follow the track through a gateway and meet a junction. Here turn left to follow the track down towards the river and the bridge that crosses it. **GR 862 294.**

6. It's here, at the bridge, where you meet the Pennine Way which is now followed back to Bowlees. Cross the bridge and at the junction on the other side turn left to follow the track up to Cronkley Farm. Just in front of the farm turn right through a small gate onto a permissive path that guides you round the buildings rather than going through the farmyard. Follow the well-marked path down through a series of gates and then up through the short but steep climb up High Crag.

When you get to the top you'll come to the side of a fence which you follow to come to a wall and stile. Cross and follow the paved path on the other side to come to another wall and gate. Again, go through and continue on the paved path to come to a fence and stile. Cross the stile and follow the path up the rise and when you get to the top you'll come to two carved marker stones indicating the route of the Pennine Way (PW) and the Green Trod (GT). Follow the green path that bears left (Pennine Way) and heads down towards what is left of an old railway wagon.

Approaching the two marker stones and, inset, the Pennine Way stone.

The path now heads down to the side of the river passing through an area of small juniper trees. This part of Teesdale forms part of what is England's largest juniper forest and is an area of international importance. Many of the trees are fenced in groups with anti-rabbit fencing to protect them.

The path crosses a small stream by some stepping stones and then as you approach two footbridges, you'll pass on the left of a ring of stones. **GR 867 281.**

On the left side of the path, just as you approach the first bridge over the Skyer Beck, stands a large mound covered in grass and juniper bushes. It's not immediately obvious from the side facing the path but if you go round the mound to the side facing the river, where the surface has been eroded, then it is possible to see that the mound is made up of iron slag. Produced as a waste product from iron smelting, this slag will have just been dumped where it was made and is evidence that the local inhabitants of the upper dale were, on a small scale, both mining and producing iron and was one of a number of sites along the river. It is not known when this process was in operation although it is probably early medieval or from an even earlier date. The site is part of a scheduled ancient monument. It is possible to touch and hold pieces of the slag and it is an unusual experience being able to touch and hold something that is 800 years old or even older. However, please leave any pieces of the slag in place and don't remove.

As you approach the bridge over the Skyer Beck the mound of iron slag is on the left underneath the juniper bushes and, inset, a piece of iron slag.

7. Cross the two footbridges and continue to follow the well-walked path. It's not long before you pass a warning sign about blasting at the quarry on the other side of the river, which is incidentally Force Garth Quarry along whose access road you walked earlier in the day.

Just after passing the sign, you'll come to a large boulder standing on the right of the path, if you look further to the right you'll see that the ground is littered with stones. These are worth a quick look as they are the remains of an ancient settlement. **GR 871 280.**

A few metres away from the 'Danger-Blasting' sign, on the left behind the fence and next to the river, lies the remains of a small stone rectangular building. The outline of the stones suggest that the building may have contained two small rooms. The building is thought to be the remains of a medieval shieling dating back to sometime between 1066 to 1540. A shieling was a seasonal structure that was used as a base where livestock would be moved up from the lower valley for the rich summer grazing on these higher pastures. The shieling would be repaired from any damage that had occurred while it was unoccupied during the winter and then it would serve as home during the summer for the herders who accompanied the livestock. There are traces of a wall attached to the main building which probably formed a small yard. This structure is a scheduled ancient monument.

The remains of the ancient shieling.

To the right of the blasting sign and stretching almost down to Blea Beck, including the lower slopes of the hillside, lie a number of even earlier settlements. The level land in front contains the remains of a number of low stone walls and the foundations of hut circles. Theses mark the site of a prehistoric settlement and may be as much as 4,000 years old.

Further up the side of the hill, on a level platform before the hill starts to climb proper, stands the remains of a rectangular building with a small pile of iron slag. A large number of the stones from the building have, over the years, been removed to help build the nearby stone walls. As the iron slag would suggest, this site is thought to be a metalworking site from the medieval period. This

The stone walls of the prehistoric settlement and, inset, the remains of the medieval building.

area of ground encompassing these settlements is a scheduled ancient monument and protected by law.

8. Continue along the path and cross the footbridge over the Blea Beck which gives a good view of Bleabeck Force, your second waterfall of the day. The path now follows the side of the river and after a little while approaches the top of the High Force waterfall, if water levels are high then you wouldn't miss the noise of falling water. Go through the gate and into the juniper woods to follow the path past the falls, at this point the views of the fall are obscured by the vegetation. Within a couple of hundred metres you'll come to a junction with a path on the left that leads to a black fence structure, follow this path through the fence to the High Force viewpoint that looks up the river to the falls.

Return back to the main path and continue along it through the low juniper trees. After a short while the trees start to end and not long after this, you'll come to a junction where the main path becomes paved and bears left steeply downhill to the side of the river and Holwick Head Bridge. **GR 889 283.**

9. Don't cross the bridge but continue following the path down the right side of the river. This obvious path is now followed downstream while the river alongside flows over it's rocky bed. The river is followed for just over a mile until you pass a carved sheep sculpture and the top of Low Force. Just after this you'll arrive at the Wynch Bridge. **GR 904 279.**

The elegant Wynch Bridge has crossed this gorge over the Tees since 1830 but this was not the first bridge on this spot. The earlier bridge was built in 1704 and was said to be the first suspension bridge in Europe. It was built to enable miners from Holwick to cross and work in the lead mines on the north side of the river. However, in 1802 it collapsed while three miners were crossing, hurtling all three into the gorge below. Sadly one of the three perished but the other two were able to be rescued however it was not until twenty-eight years later that the new chain suspension bridge replaced the earlier ill-fated one.

10. Cross the bridge, taking notice about the sign saying one at a time, and follow the path through the wood up to a gate and stile. Cross the stile and then follow the path over two fields to come to the roadside. Taking care, cross the road and turn right to go up the lane opposite, at the head of which stands the Bowlees Visitor Centre. Now you can pay a visit to the café and a well earned cuppa and maybe even a little morsel to top-up the depleted energy levels. From the Visitor Centre, you just need to retrace your steps back to the car park.

Electricity poles crossing Widdybank Pasture. The floats warn grouse of the existence of the wires. Walk 8: Langdon Beck and Widdybank Pastures.

WALK 8: LANGDON BECK & WIDDYBANK PASTURES

A walk into the wide open spaces of the upper dale and one that when walked in the winter months can really demonstrate the open, wild aspects of the upper reaches of this valley. Along the way you'll come across what is called a multi-period ancient monument, an earthwork that was used through a number of time periods. You'll also come across a little known lead mine and, hopefully, you'll not have an encounter with a fearsome water hag.

DISTANCE: 6.8 mile / 10.9 km
ASCENT: 541 feet / 165 metres
TERRAIN: The walk does tend to split about 50/50 over walking on track and walking over rough pasture. In and after periods of wet weather there are patches where the pasture can get wet underfoot but by following the guide and using common sense, then you can normally miss the worst of these. The majority of the climbing on this route is in the early stages when you are heading up from the car park and is more of a steady climb than steep.
TIME: 4 to 4½ hours
START: Hanging Shaw car park. GR NY 867 298.
MAP: OL31 North Pennines. Teesdale and Weardale.
ACCESS: The route is all on public rights of way.
DOGS: As the route is all on public rights of way, then dogs are allowed. However, as this route crosses Moor House National Nature Reserve then they must be kept on a lead at all times. Livestock, including sheep, cattle and horses will be encountered throughout the route and in addition, as the route does pass through a couple of farmyards, then farm dogs will also probably be encountered. There are also quite a number of high stiles on this walk that will require you to lift your dog over.

Grid References

Car park	867 298
Track crossroads	869 309
Lead mine	862 311
Langdon Beck Inn	853 312
Road/track junction	847 309
Widdy Bank Farm	837 298
Saur Hill Bridge	855 302
Cronkley Bridge	862 293
Car park	867 298

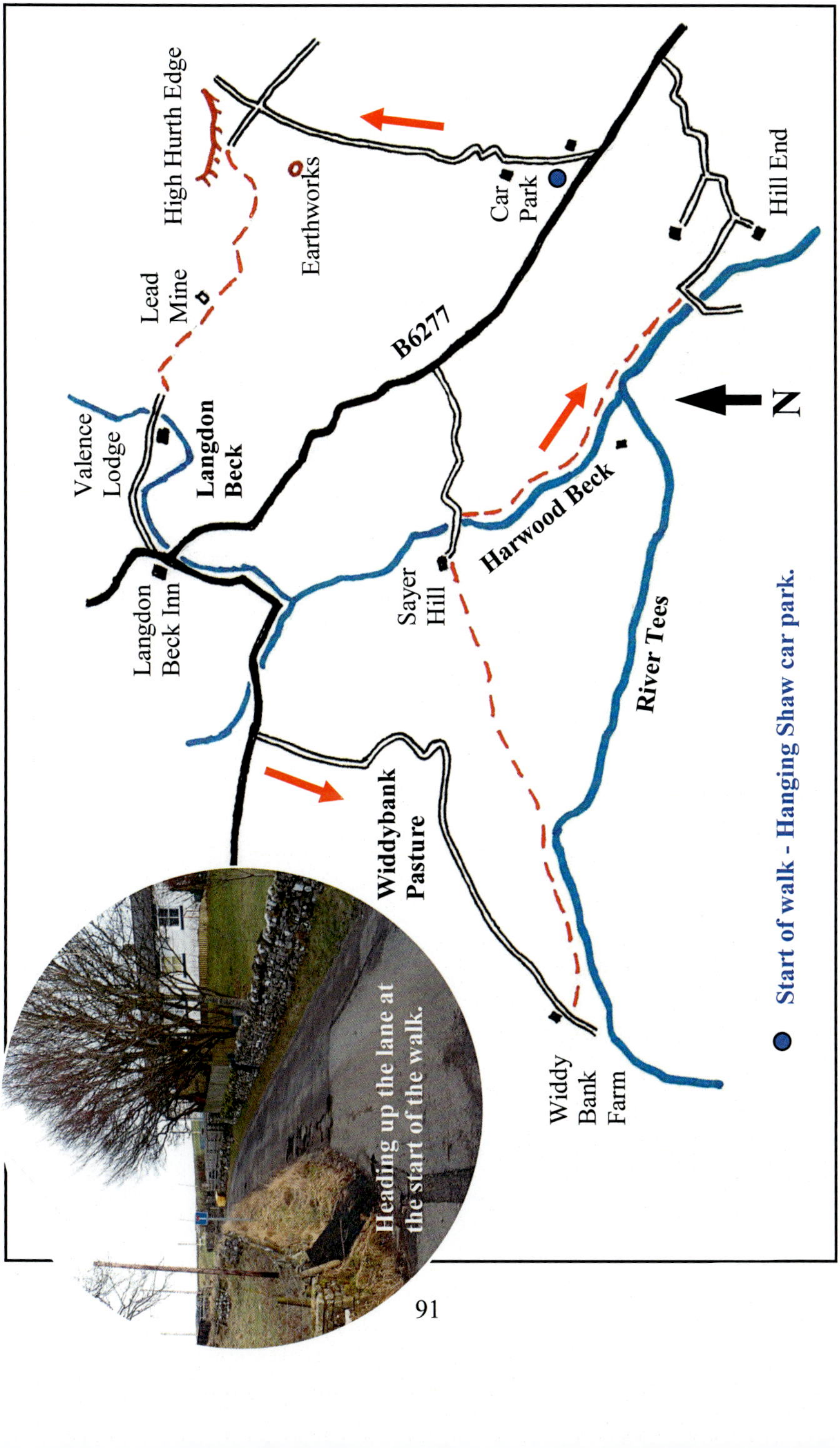

Heading up the lane at the start of the walk.

FGS Grading
Grading is F4 [D1, N1, T1, R1, H0]

Distance	**1**	6 – 12 miles
Navigation	**1**	Basic navigation skills needed
Terrain	**1**	50 – 75% on graded track or path 25 – 50% off track
Remoteness	**1**	Countryside in fairly close proximity to habitation – at least 80% of the route within 2 miles
Height	**0**	Less than 100 ft per mile

THE WALK

1. From the car park, head up the lane, past the school and through the gateway to Rose Tree Farm. There is no waymarker on the gate but it is a right of way. Follow the track and when you get to the farm go between the buildings and then turn right and continue up the hill. The track now twists and turns a bit as it climbs up the slope passing through four fields. As you near the end of the fourth field there is a large flat area on the left.

The large flat area on the left side of the field.

The large raised, flat area to the left of the track is actually the remains of a prehistoric cemetery, presumed to be Neolithic, around 4,000 years old. The mound is roughly 55 metres long (180 feet) and 8 metres (26 feet) wide, now it only stands at a height of half a metre but in the past it may have been considerably higher. On the eastern side of the mound, a circular enclosure has been laid on top of the mound, this is early medieval, which began at the end of the 4th century in the years following the departure of the Romans, and is part of a farmstead that existed here and which may also explain the reduction in the height of the mound.

In 1978 the area was excavated and it was found that the spine of the mound was marked by an irregular double-row of flat stone slabs. Items recovered from this area of the excavation were mainly flints, mostly small waste flakes although there was a number of worked items and also included a possible perforated stone macehead.

The circular enclosure built on top of the mound measures 15 metres (49 feet) across it's internal diameter and has the traces of an enclosing ditch on it's southern side. With the early medieval period starting at the end of the 4th century, then it is possible but far from certain that the circle may be the foundations of a round house. These buildings were a very good and practical design and their use extended from the prehistoric well into the years after the Romans left. They were also known to incorporate drainage ditches round the outside of their walls.

The area of the mound and farmstead are a scheduled ancient monument.

The circular enclosure and, inset, two sections of the walls.

Return back to the track and go through the gate and after several metres the track comes to a crossroads. After bad weather the crossroads may be a bit churned up by quad bikes but it is still easily identifiable. **GR 870 309.**

2. At the crossroads, the main track turns right but don't follow this. Instead turn left and follow the minor branch as it heads towards the cliffs of High Hurth Edge. Underneath the cliffs, the track comes to both a gate and a kissing gate in the stone wall.

The cliffs of High Hurth Edge.

The cliffs of High Hurth Edge hide the only cave system within the dale. At first glance these look like no more than small cracks in the face of the crag, however, once in then the entrances do become larger and are capable of being pot-holed. Not that you'd get me into them, my family spent far too many generations trying to get out of the pits just to have me start going back underground as a hobby.

Its not just us humans that have used these caves as within them the bones of lynx have been discovered. This large cat was a native of these dales in prehistoric times but became extinct in this country long before the Roman invasion, probably dying out between 10,000 BC and AD43.

Go through the gate and head across the next field bearing slightly to the left to go down the slope. As you cross the field you'll see what appears to be a number of gates in the wall on the opposite side. Head for the upper gate and as you get closer you'll notice that most of these gates are in the bottom, left-hand wall of the field. When you get to the upper gate you'll find that it is a double-gate, one after the other, with no waymarker to indicate that you actually go through them.

Despite this, go through and then immediately turn left to follow the wall across a shallow dip in the ground and onto the following rise. Here turn right to head straight across the field, following the low ridge, to a wooden stile in the fence on the opposite side. A ruined stone wall immediately behind the stile helps to identify it.

If you choose, you can head straight for the stile when you exit the double-gate but you'll have to cross an extensive bog area. It's much easier to follow the wall and stay to the slightly higher ground.

Cross the stile and you'll find that the ruined stone wall is really the remains of a small stone building. Look to the right and you'll see the entrance to a lead level. **GR 862 312.**

The entrance to the adit, or level, is part of the High Hurth Edge network of mines, the majority of which sit a short distance to the north on and above the cliff face that can be seen there. Constructed during the height of the lead mining era in Teesdale, during the 1700's, the level was used to access the lower levels of the lead vein as it ran from the cliff edge. Most lead veins ran in vertical lines rather than horizontal, as the minerals crystallised in the faults between the rocks. This meant that the miners could work the full height of the vein, accessing it from different points as the fall in the landscape allowed.

3. From the mine, follow the faint path that heads towards a belt of trees, making your way across the slope of the hill, and slowly descending towards a visible gate in the bottom wall of the field. When you get there, you'll find that the gate is waymarked, so go through and follow the track straight ahead and then right to follow it down to the buildings of Valence Lodge. Cross the bridge over the Langdon Beck and then bear right to go between the buildings to enter the yard. Here turn left to

Following the path away from the mine towards the belt of trees and, inset, the Langdon Beck Inn.

follow the track through the gateway and stay on it as it runs alongside and above the beck to eventually come to the roadside opposite the Langdon Beck Inn. **GR 853 312.**

4. At the road turn left to reluctantly go past the pub and then turn right to follow the minor road signposted to Cow Green Reservoir. Follow the road as it goes through the scattered houses of Langdon Beck keeping the beck itself, on the left-hand side. After a short distance, you'll come to the point where the waters of the Langdon Beck flow into those of the Harwood Beck and here the road turns sharply right.

Ignore the concrete causeway that goes straight ahead over the Harwood Beck and continue to follow the road as it turns right to come to a bridge over the beck. Go over, stay on the road and after a short distance you'll come to a cattle grid. A few minutes later you'll come to a second cattle grid just in front of a white building on the right side of the road, and here on the left of the road is a footpath marker post, a gate and a smaller pedestrian gate. **GR 847 309.**

5. Don't cross the cattle grid but instead turn left to leave the road and go through the gate. Ignore the bridleway marker that goes off to the left and continue following the track straight ahead as it crosses Widdybank Pasture.

The track is followed for quite a while, going through a number of gateways before starting a slow descent down the low ridge towards the River Tees and the white-washed buildings of Widdy Bank Farm. After crossing a cattle grid next to a small barn, the track eventually arrives in the yard in front of the farm buildings. **GR 837 298.**

Following the track across Widdybank Pastures and, inset, approaching Widdy Bank Farm.

The farm itself is the headquarters of the Moor House Nature Reserve and a comfortable wooden bench at the front of the buildings makes a nice spot for a lunch break. And while you are sat having a cuppa, if you look to your left, eastwards, you'll see a nick in the distant skyline that is Coldberry Gutter, visited on an earlier walk and visible from many places within the dale.

6. Continue on the track to go through the farm and as it goes through the following field you'll see that it heads towards a gateway. Don't follow the track all the way to the gate, a hundred metres or so before you get to it, turn left to go up and over a gated stile built into the left-hand wall. The stile leads you onto a distinctive riverside path.

Follow the path downstream next to the river, passing a number of marker posts and going over a couple of stiles as you go. Eventually you'll come to the point where the river bends to the right and the riverbank becomes too steep to follow and here the path climbs up the bank above the river. At the top of the rise, the path continues straight ahead while the river bends away to the right making the path head across the field.

Although not showing any markers, this is the well-walked Pennine Way and the path is quite distinctive. In places there are small stone flags to help with erosion control and in the boggier places, duckboards to stop you sinking too far into the peat. The path crosses a couple of stiles as it crosses the pastures. The last stile being a little way up from a tree next to the wall, here cross the stile and continue straight ahead, keeping the wire fence on your left, to pass the farm of Sayer Hill and come to a track. Turn right to follow the track the short distance down to Saur Hill Bridge which crosses our old friend, the Harwood Beck. **GR 855 302.**

7. Cross the bridge and immediately turn right through the small gate to follow the Pennine Way downstream next to the beck. After about 800/900 metres you'll come to the confluence of the Harwood Beck and the River Tees. At this point the Tees is only marginally the larger water course.

The confluence of the Tees and the Harwood Beck.

Continue to follow the side of the river downstream to come to Cronkley Bridge. **GR 862 294.**

8. Don't cross the bridge but instead turn left to follow the track away from the river. After around 20 metres the track bends right to go through a gateway and then climbs up a bank to another gateway and just after that a junction that leads to Hill End. Turn left to continue heading away from the river.

You'll soon pass through another gateway before arriving at another junction. Here bear right and after passing through yet another gateway, you'll eventually come to the roadside of the B6277.

As you head towards the road, you'll pass a tall upright stone standing on the right side of the track. This is the third of the three stones from the Time Sculpture which is based in the picnic area of the Hanging Shaw car park.

Turn left onto the road and follow it for a few hundred metres to come back to the car park which lies on the right side of the road.

PEG POWLER'S SUDS

If you go down to the Tees today ....

Keep your eyes open for the whitey-brown foam building up on the surface and if you see it .... keep well away from the water's edge.

Peg Powler is not a nice creature. A green haired, snaggle-toothed water hag that lives below the surface of the river and preys upon the unwary, dragging them down into the depths and a watery death. For generations Teesdale folk have kept their children in check with tales of Peg and her fondness for naughty children who would suddenly disappear if they got too close to the water's edge.

Peg roams the length of the river, over the centuries taking victims from the upper reaches all the way down to Piercebridge. Her presence being indicated by the whitey-brown foam on the surface of the river caused by her passage under the water and known locally as Peg Powler's Suds.

Since the building of Cow Green Reservoir and it's dam in the 1960's, Peg has been relatively quiet but she is not gone ...... only sleeping.

As you walk along the river's edge and the foam rises then be careful. If you suddenly feel a hand around your ankle and you then look down into the face of an old hag with long, unkempt green hair billowing across the water then you've met Peg. Struggle as much as you like, her grip is like iron and she'll slowly drag you under to your doom.

The prehistoric enclosure of Grey Stones and, inset, crossing the Gill Beck.
Walk 9: Banks of the Greta and Grey Stones.

WALK 9: BANKS OF THE GRETA AND GREY STONES

Teesdale was described by Wainwright in his book on the Pennine Way as 'sylvan' mainly due to the trees lining the river on it's journey upstream from Middleton. However, there are small parts of Teesdale where the ancient woodland that once cloaked the entire country still exists. As in most parts these woods survive in the steep-sided valleys of rivers and streams where the land couldn't be put to a more productive use and has, in the main, just been left.

This walk follows one of these stretches of woodland, this one lining the side of the River Greta, a tributary of the Tees. Although not necessarily an easy walk, this stretch along the banks of the Greta rewards the effort by being one of the best woodland walks in the county and definitely gives a sense of exploring the ancient wild wood of folklore. As you leave the woodland, you'll pass the remains of a small medieval castle that was the centre of the settlements along the Greta during the Middle Ages. Later in the walk, evidence of another settlement is uncovered, this one going further back in time to before the arrival of the upstarts from Italy, the Romans, on these shores.

DISTANCE: 6.6 mile / 10.6 km
ASCENT: 650 feet / 198 metres
TERRAIN: In the main, this walk encompasses field and woodland paths with a stretch along a very quiet country lane. However, the woods in question border the edge of the steep-sided Greta valley and in a number of places go down to the riverside and then come back up again. Some of these climbs and descents, although not long, are quite steep and in places there is a bit of exposure, a steep drop down into the valley on one side of the path. There are also two stream crossings on this walk both of which do not use a bridge. In times of bad weather or high water levels it would be advisable not to do this walk.
TIME: 4½ to 5 hours
START: The village of Barningham. There is a long green on one side of the road as you pass through the village and there is ample road-side parking either next to the green or outside the houses on the opposite side of the road. However, please don't park on the green itself or inconvenience local residents. GR GR NZ 084 103.
MAP: OL30 Yorkshire Dales - Northern and Central Areas.
ACCESS: The route is all on public rights of way apart from a short diversion over access land to visit the prehistoric settlement of Grey Stones.
DOGS: As the route is all public rights of way, then dogs are allowed. However, be aware that there are sections of this walk, as it goes through the woods bordering the River Greta, that have a steep drop to one side down to the river.

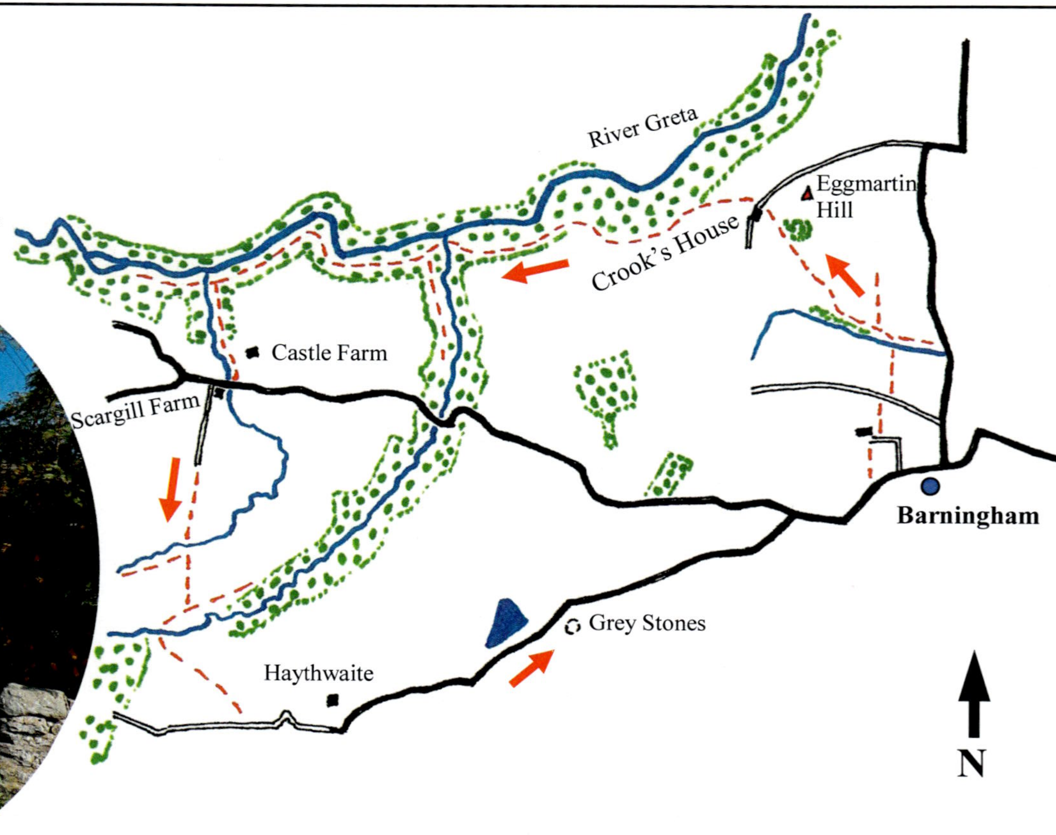

Heading down Shaw Lane at the start of the walk.

In addition, you are quite likely to meet cattle, including a bull, in the fields surrounding Scargill Farm.

Grid References

Barningham village green	084 103
Footbridge	082 109
Crook's House	076 115
Path junction	061 112
Footbridge	051 111
Path/road junction	053 106
Gate	051 099
Top of bank	051 096
Gate	049 090
Settlement	068 095
Barningham village green	084 103

FGS Grading

Grading is T5 [D1, N1, T2, R1, H0]

Distance	**1**	6 – 12 miles
Navigation	**1**	Basic navigation skills needed
Terrain	**2**	25 -50% on graded track or path, 50 – 75% off track
Remoteness	**1**	Countryside in fairly close proximity to habitation – at least 80% of the route within 2 miles
Height	**0**	Less than 100 ft per mile

THE WALK

1. Head westward through the village following the right-side of the road as it slowly climbs up the bank. As you get to the end of the village green, you'll come to a track just after you have passed Shaw House, the name is on the gate to the cottage, with a footpath sign pointing up it. The track is called, appropriately enough, Shaw Lane.

Turn right here to leave the road and follow the track between the houses. Once behind the buildings, continue straight ahead ignoring the tracks to either side. The track continues between the fields and then starts to bend to the left and approaches Bank's House.

This is the start of the far-reaching views out and across the valley of the Tees, an element that is encountered through much of the walk.

Just in front of the house, turn right through a waymarked gateway to cross what can only be described as part of the house's garden and head to a visible stile a short distance away that leads into a field. Continue straight ahead, following the hedge on the right, to come to another stile in the bottom wall of the field. Cross and, again, continue straight down the field to the next stile which stands to the right of the gate.

Heading down across the fields.

Cross the stile into a lane and here turn right to follow the lane for 25 metres until you come to a stile in the left-hand wall. The stile is not marked and can easily be missed but it stands just behind a large tree. Go over the stile and follow the left-hand wall and hedge down to a footbridge over the Nor Beck. **GR 082 109.**

2. Once on the other side of the bridge, follow the left-hand fence as it skirts round some low trees, roughly following the course of the beck upstream. After a little distance the fence ends and the path follows the stream, albeit a little distance away from it, to come to a gate.

This gate has the largest and heaviest gate hook that I have ever seen, if that is what is needed to keep the gates closed then the sheep around here must have been on a body-building course.

The rough track leading to the small patch of trees and, inset, the biggest gate hook that I have ever seen.

Continue ahead for a short distance to come to a rough track that goes through a gateway into a small patch of trees next to the beck. Follow the track and after about 100 metres you'll exit through a waymarked gate into a field. Here head diagonally right across the field, making for the buildings of Crooks House.

As you make your way up the field, you'll find that you are crossing a number of undulations in the ground surface. These are the remains of medieval rigg and furrow ploughing.

Just before you get to the buildings, go through a waymarked gate next to the left corner of a small wood and then head to the right of the buildings to come to a farm track. **GR 076 115.**

3. Go straight across the farm track and up another track on the opposite side which bends to the left around a small patch of trees and comes to a waymarked gate leading into a field. Once in the field, follow the right-hand fence to come to the side of a wood. Continue to follow the fence with now, both it and the wood on your right.

Eventually you'll come to the end of the field where you'll find a rough track and two gateways. Go through the right-hand gate with the small yellow 'Please shut the gate' sign to enter the wood.

Follow the path as it continues to run next to the fence although now with it on your left. Within a few metres you'll come to a junction and here continue straight ahead following the fence and ignore the path going downhill to the right.

There now follows one of the most pleasant woodland walks in the county. After a while you'll pass a small barn over in the field on the left and the path now starts a long descent down into the valley of the River Greta. As you descend you'll pass a waymarker post, which provides a measure of reassurance that you

Following the side of the fence.

are on the right path, and shortly after this, the path starts to descend a lot more steeply. At the bottom of the bank you come to the junction where the Gill Beck flows into the River Greta.

Cross the beck, this is a little bit tricky but the short scramble down the bank to the side of the beck is actually easier than it first seems and at the time of test walking the stones across the beck were quite safe and secure. Once on the other side, follow the path steeply up the opposite bank to come to a waymarked junction at the top of the gorge. **GR 061 112.**

4. Ignore the left-hand branch and continue to follow the path straight ahead as it runs high above the River Greta. The path through the woods is now quite undulating as it alternates between going down to the side of the river and running high above it. At times the climbs and descents are quite steep and there is one particular stretch beside the river where you have to pick your way through a jumble of rocks. However, after following the path for just over 1 km you'll come to the point where the Gregory Beck joins the Greta and just a few metres up the course of the beck you'll come to a footbridge. **GR 051 111.**

5. Don't turn right to cross the bridge but instead continue straight ahead following the path next to the beck as it makes it's way through Henning Wood. The path goes slowly uphill as it makes it's way and finally comes to a gate leading into a field.

Go through and follow the sunken, grassy track uphill to come to a second way-marked gate. Go through and, ignoring Castle Farm on the left, immediately turn right to head for a stone stile in the wall just a little distance to the left of the bridge over the Gregory Beck. The stile leads onto Chapel Lane. **GR 053 106.**

6. Turn right to follow Chapel Lane for 100 metres until you come to a bridleway on the left that goes up through the yard of Scargill Farm to a gate on the right of some barns. Go through the gate and follow the track straight ahead for around 350 metres. Be aware that at the time of test walking, the narrow field that the track runs through contained cattle including a very large but extremely docile bull.

When you get to the end of the field, the way ahead is blocked by a number of animal pens but the track bears right to go through a gate and then continues straight ahead but now with the fence on your left. When the hard-core surface of the track ends, it continues but more as a grass track. Follow it as it goes over the rise and then heads downhill but bearing slightly to the right, to come to a

Passing by the side of the animal pens.

waymarked gate at the bottom of the field. **GR 051 099.**

7. Go through the gate and cross the infant Gregory Beck, the same one that you followed up from the River Greta. Keep going straight ahead following a faint continuation of the track and after 400 metres you'll come to a steep bank above the Gill Beck. **GR 051 096.**

Heading down the sunken track towards the stream crossing and, inset, the new small bridleway sign.

8. Follow the top of the bank round to the right until you come to a sunken track that heads down to the beck and a visible gate in the wall on the opposite side. Head down to the beck and when you get there, rather than cross where the bank is steep, head to the left where there is a single tree, the crossing is much easier here.

Once across, go through the gate and follow the path as it heads up the side of the hill through the newly planted saplings. The path bears to the left and comes to a new, small bridleway sign. This now directs you to the right and along a wide avenue-style gap between the rows of tree plantings.

Follow this 'avenue' and after a short while you'll come to a dried up stream bed with the remains of an old rotten tree on the left. Here, go straight across the stream bed to continue following the 'avenue' as it starts to bear right to go up the hillside and eventually come to a wooden gate in a wire fence. **GR 049 090.**

Note that the route through this new plantation does not strictly tie-in with

that shown on the OS map but it seems to be the preferred route between the saplings.

9. Go through the gate onto a track and turn left to follow it. After a while you'll pass a stile on the left with a bridleway marker which is where the bridleway is supposed to exit. Stay on the track as it shortly bends to cross the dry ford of Scale Knoll Gill and then does a short climb up to a gate.

Go through the gate and pass the entrance to the farm of Haythwaite. Here the track gains a tarmac surface and you are now walking along what is a narrow road. This is not as bad as it sounds as, being a dead-end road, it is very quiet and the views on the left, out and over the Tees valley are outstanding.

Stay on the road until you pass a reservoir a short distance away on the left. Now as you walk along the road, on the hillside in front, facing you on the right side of the road and clearly visible lies a group of large stones. Known as the Grey Stones, the stones laid across the hillside are the remains of a prehistoric settlement. The road now passes over two small streams before starting to bend to the left. From this point it is an easy enough diversion to the stones which only lie 100 metres off the right side of the road. **GR 068 095.**

Approaching the Grey Stones which lie 100 metres on the right side of the road on the side of the hill and, inset, the first view of the stones.

10. After visiting the settlement, return to the road and continue your journey along it. When you come to a road junction on the outskirts of Barningham, turn right to follow the road back down into the village and return to the car.

GREY STONES

Sited on the low hills on the south side of the road, the group of boulders called Grey Stones on the OS map are actually the remains of a small prehistoric enclosure, very probably used to hold livestock.

The enclosure is one of a number of prehistoric sites located across these hills. These sites include hut circles, stone walls, cairns, small enclosures, cup and ring marked stones, known as rock art, and even a stone circle.

Then, as now, the land here leads into the Stainmore Gap, the natural pass that cuts through the Pennines. Below you lies the A66, one of the main trans-Pennine routes in the north which itself follows the route of the old Roman road through the gap in the Pennines.

It is thought by many archaeologists that the hillside above you formed part of a prehistoric routeway through the Pennines, going through the Stainmore Gap and linking the prehistoric monuments lower down, in the Vale of Mowbray, to similar monuments in Cumbria, in particular to those in the Penrith area.

Evidence exists to prove that long distance trade and travel were part of everyday life in the prehistoric, axes made from stone quarried in Langdale in the Lake District have been found the length and breadth of the country and even on the continent. So the possibility of a pilgrimage being made from a ritual or sacred site on one side of the Pennines to another on the other side is not unrealistic.

Grey Stones, as with some of the other sites on this moor, was probably seasonal. Only being used during the summer months when man ventured up from the lower plains. In this he would be both hunter and gatherer, hunting the upland game and bringing his livestock to graze on the summer pastures.

Grey Stones standing on the hillside and, inset, some of the stones that formed the enclosure walls.

APPENDIX

Ferguson Grading System (`FGS`)

1. Introduction
The FGS has been adopted as a means of assessing the nature and severity of the various walks in this book and the abilities and equipment needed to tackle each one safely. The FGS was developed by Stuart Ferguson, a long time fell and trail runner, climber, mountaineer, mountain-biker and general outdoor enthusiast. In the opinion of Trailguides, the FGS is the most accurate and comprehensive grading system for comparing off-road walking, running and mountain-biking routes anywhere in the country.

2. The System
Tables 1 & 2, set out below, are used in order to give a grading to each route. Table 1 sets out three categories of country that a route could potentially cross, together with a range of factors that would need to be considered when tackling that route. The three categories are, Trail, Fell and Mountain, and after assessing which category best fits the route, a letter, either `T`, `F` or `M`, is allocated to that route. Where a route does not fit perfectly into one of the three categories the closest category is allocated.

Table 2 deals with five specific aspects of the route, distance, navigation, terrain, remoteness and height gain, and each one is allocated a letter, `D`, `N`, `T`, `R`, and `H`. Each letter is also given a severity score from the range 0-3 or 0-4, in respect of distance (`D`). The higher the number, the more severe the route. The five severity scores are then added together to give an overall score. The overall score is then put with the Table 1 category letter (i.e. `T`, `F` or `M`).

In order to show how the grading has been determined for each walk in this book, the five individual severity scores are set out, in square brackets, immediately after the actual grading. So, for example, Walk 8 Langdon Beck & Widdybank Pastures has a grading of F4 [D1, N1, T1, R1, H0], indicating that it is a Fell Category walk with a total severity score of 4. This is made up of the five specific severity scores, for distance (`D`), navigation (`N`), terrain (`T`), remoteness (`R`) and height gain (`H`), of 1, 1, 1, 1 and 0 respectively. The highest total severity score which can be achieved is 16 and the lowest total severity score achievable is 0.

The table which accompanies the grading for each walk sets out the specific factors, extracted from Table 2, that need to be considered when tackling that particular walk.

TABLE 1

	TRAIL	**FELL**	**MOUNTAIN**
Description	Lowland and forest areas including urban, cultivated and forested locations.	Moorlands and upland areas which may include some upland cultivated and forestry areas plus possibly remote locations.	Upland and mountain areas including remote and isolated locations.
Height	Not usually above 1,000 feet but may go up to 2,500 feet	Usually above 1,000 feet, up to 2,500 feet and above.	Usually above 2,500 feet and up to 4,000 feet.
Way-marking	Usually	Limited	None
Terrain	Usually graded paths, tracks and trails but may include some off-trail	May include some graded paths, tracks and trails but mainly off-trail	Virtually all off-trail
Height gain	Limited height gain	May include considerable height gain	May include some severe height gain.
Effects of weather	Very limited effect	May be prone to sudden weather changes	Extreme weather a possibility
Navigational skills	None to basic	Basic to competent	Competent to expert
Equipment	Walking shoes/boots. Possibly waterproofs Food and drink dependant upon route.	3/4 season walking boots. Full waterproof cover. Possibly map and compass dependant upon route. Food and drink dependant upon route.	Mountain boots. Full waterproof cover. Map and compass. Food and drink
Escape Routes	Yes	Some	Some to nil

TABLE 2

Score	0	1	2	3	4
Distance	Up to 6 miles	6 – 12 miles	12 – 18 miles	18 miles +	24 miles +
Navigation	No navigation skills needed	Basic navigation skills needed	Competent navigation skills needed	Expert navigation skills needed	
Terrain	75% + on graded track or path	50 – 75% on graded track or path 25 – 50% off track	25 -50% on graded track or path 50 – 75% off track	Under 25% on graded track or path Over 75% off track	
Remoteness	Urban	Countryside in fairly close proximity to habitation – at least 80% of the route within 2 miles	Countryside not in close proximity to habitation – less than 20% of the route within 2 miles	Remote, isolated location	
Height gain	Less than 100 ft per mile	Over 100 ft per mile	Over 125 ft per mile	Over 250 ft per mile	

Notes to Table 2

Graded paths = Well established paths with a stable surface.

Escape routes = The opportunity to cut the route short and return to the start without completing the full course in the event of weather changes or unforeseen incidents.

The Author

Keven Shevels

Kev has been involved with outdoor sports for over forty years since his school days doing the Duke of Edinburgh award, spending his time either walking, running and latterly mountain biking through the countryside of the North East and beyond. He is not ashamed to admit that he is one of these boring people who can sit and spend hours reading a map the way that other people read a book.

His great delight is coming up with new routes that he can subsequently explore and investigate especially if he can couple this with his interest in history, in particular the prehistoric. This usually means much more than a walk as his routes tend to take a view not only on the landscape but also its relationship with events and occurrences that have happened in the past. In many ways this curiosity and knowledge of the Durham Dales can make him a perfect guide to this undervalued part of our region.

Now in his fifties, Kev has been unable to continue his running due to injury problems but instead has been co-author of one of the most innovative series of coaching books for fell and trail runners in recent years. He now brings his easy to read, informative style of writing to guide books for those who walk in the countryside of County Durham, his home county.

The author having a break out in the Durham countryside.

Walking North East

Walking North East is the brand name for the walking publications produced by Trailguides and reflects the pride that we, as North Easterners, have in our countryside, our history and our culture. Based in Darlington, we are a small independent publisher specialising in guidebooks centred on the North Eastern counties of England. Our target is to produce guides that are as user-friendly, easy to use and provide as much information as possible and all in an easily readable format. In essence to increase the enjoyment of the user and to showcase the very best of the great North Eastern countryside. Our series of books explores the heritage of us all and lets you see your region with new eyes, these books are written to not just take you on a walk but to investigate, explore and understand the objects, places and history that has shaped not just the countryside but also the people of this corner of England.

If you've enjoyed following the routes in this guide and want news and details of other publications that are being developed under the Walking North East label then look at the company website at **www.trailguides.co.uk**

Comments and, yes, criticisms, are always welcomed especially if you discover a change to a route. Contact us by email through the website or by post at Trailguides Limited, 35 Carmel Road South, Darlington, Co Durham DL3 8DQ.

Other walking books from Walking North East.
At the time of publication the following books are also available but with new titles being regularly added to our publication list, keep checking our website. All of these publications can be purchased as books or downloads from our website.

Northumberland.
The Cheviot Hills.
Walks from Wooler.
The Hills of Upper Coquetdale.
Walks from Kirknewton.
Walks on the Wild Side: The Cheviot Hills.
Walks Around Rothbury and Coquetdale.
Walks in Hadrian's Wall Country,

County Durham.
Hamsterley Forest.
The Barningham Trail.
Ancient Stones.
Walks from Stanhope.
Mid-Teesdale Walks.
Walking in Weardale.
Walking in Teesdale

North Yorkshire.
Walking the Hills of Upper Swaledale.
Walks Around Gunnerside.
Walks around Reeth and Upper Swaledale.
Walking around Osmotherley and the Cleveland Hills

Have a look at our Facebook page - **Walking North East** for current news on ourselves and our publications. The page also contains news, views and articles on all aspects of walking within the North Eastern counties of Cleveland, Durham, Northumberland and North Yorkshire. Definitely well worth a look and clicking the Like button.

For those that don't have or want to use Facebook then why not subscribe to our monthly newsletter. Titled 'Walking North East' this contains the same news, views and articles as our Facebook page. Subscriptions are free with no obligation to purchase and can be made via our website at www.trailguides.co.uk . Previous issues of Walking North East can also be accessed free via the website.

Acknowledgements.
As always a book is never written in isolation and so thanks are due to Harry Manuel for accompanying me on these walks and helping with the route testing and proof reading. He also has the misfortune to occasionally appear as the "model" in some of the photographs. Thanks are also due to my wife Lyn for the patience and tolerance shown while I "disappear" to walk and write about these routes and also her help in pulling the final book together.

Disclaimer

The information contained in these pages and the route descriptions is provided in good faith, but no warranty is made for its accuracy. The contents are, at the time of writing and to the best of our knowledge, up-to-date and correct. However, the world is a changing environment and what is correct one day may not be so the next. Care should always be taken when following these route descriptions just as it should when following maps or waymarkers of any kind..

No guarantee whatsoever is provided by the author and/or Trailguides Limited and no liability is accepted for any loss, damage or injury of any kind resulting from the use of this book, nor as a result of any defect or inaccuracy in it.

As with all outdoor activities, you and you alone are responsible for your safety and well being.